Nmc/ff

The Literary Agenda

Please return / renew by date shown.
You can renew at: **norlink.norfolk.gov.uk**
or by telephone: **0344 800 8006**
Please have your library card & PIN ready.

NORFOLK LIBRARY
AND INFORMATION SERVICE

The Literary Agenda

Reading and the Reader

PHILIP DAVIS

OXFORD
UNIVERSITY PRESS

OXFORD

UNIVERSITY PRESS

Great Clarendon Street, Oxford, OX2 6DP,
United Kingdom

Oxford University Press is a department of the University of Oxford.
It furthers the University's objective of excellence in research, scholarship,
and education by publishing worldwide. Oxford is a registered trade mark of
Oxford University Press in the UK and in certain other countries

© Philip Davis 2013

The moral rights of the author have been asserted

First Edition published in 2013

Impression: 2

British Library Cataloguing in Publication Data

Data available

ISBN 978-0-19-968318-5

Printed in Great Britain by
Clays Ltd, St Ives plc

For the grandsons, Leo and Chester

Series Introduction

The Crisis in, the Threat to, the Plight of the Humanities: enter these phrases in Google's search engine and there are 23 million results, in a great fifty-year-long cry of distress, outrage, fear, and melancholy. Grant, even, that every single anxiety and complaint in that catalogue of woe is fully justified—the lack of public support for the arts, the cutbacks in government funding for the humanities, the imminent transformation of a literary and verbal culture by visual/virtual/digital media, the decline of reading...And still, though it were all true, and just because it might be, there would remain the problem of the response itself. Too often there's recourse to the shrill moan of offended piety or a defeatist withdrawal into professionalism.

The Literary Agenda is a series of short polemical monographs that believes there is a great deal that needs to be said about the state of literary education inside schools and universities and more fundamentally about the importance of literature and of reading in the wider world. The category of 'the literary' has always been contentious. What *is* clear, however, is how increasingly it is dismissed or is unrecognized as a way of thinking or an arena for thought. It is sceptically challenged from within, for example, by the sometimes rival claims of cultural history, contextualized explanation, or media studies. It is shaken from without by even greater pressures: by economic exigency and the severe social attitudes that can follow from it; by technological change that may leave the traditional forms of serious human communication looking merely antiquated. For just these reasons this is the right time for renewal, to start reinvigorated work into the meaning and value of literary reading for the sake of the future.

It is certainly no time to retreat within institutional walls. For all the academic resistance to 'instrumentalism', to governmental measurements of public impact and practical utility, literature exists in and across society. The 'literary' is not pure or specialized or self-confined; it is not restricted to the practitioner in writing or the academic in studying. It exists in the whole range of the world which is its subject matter: it consists in what non-writers actively receive from writings when, for example, they start to see the world more imaginatively as a result of reading novels and begin to think more carefully about human personality. It comes from literature making available much of human life that would not otherwise be existent to thought or recognizable as knowledge. If it is true that involvement in literature, so far from being a minority aesthetic, represents a significant contribution to the life of human thought, then that idea has to be argued at the public level without succumbing to a hollow rhetoric or bowing to a reductive world-view. Hence the effort of this series to take its place *between* literature and the world. The double-sided commitment to occupying that place and establishing its reality is the only 'agenda' here, without further prescription as to what should then be thought or done within it.

What is at stake is not simply some defensive or apologetic 'justification' in the abstract. The case as to why literature matters in the world not only has to be argued conceptually and strongly tested by thought, it should be given presence, performed, and brought to life in the way that literature itself does. That is why this series includes the writers themselves, the novelists and poets, in order to try to close the gap between the thinking of the artists and the thinking of those who read and study them. It is why it also involves other kinds of thinkers—the philosopher, the theologian, the psychologist, the neuroscientist—examining the role of literature within their own life's work and thought, and the effect of that work, in turn, upon literary thinking. This series admits and encourages personal voices in an unpredictable variety of individual approach and expression, speaking wherever possible across countries and disciplines and temperaments. It aims for something more than intellectual assent: rather the literary sense of what it is like to feel the thought, to embody an idea in a person, to bring it to being in a narrative or in aid of adventurous reflection. If the artists refer to their own works, if other thinkers return to ideas that have marked much of their working life, that is not their vanity nor a failure of originality. It is what the series has asked of them: to speak out of what they know and care about, in whatever language can best serve their most serious thinking, and without the necessity of trying to cover every issue or meet every objection in each volume.

Philip Davis

Preface

In the words of psychoanalyst W. R. Bion:

If a person cannot 'think' with his thoughts, that is to say that he has thoughts but lacks the apparatus of 'thinking' which enables him to use his thoughts, to think them as it were, then the personality is incapable of learning from experience. This failure is serious. Failure to eat, drink or breathe properly has disastrous consequences for life itself. Failure to use emotional experience produces a comparable disaster in the development of the personality.[1]

This book is about how literature helps its readers to think such thoughts, thoughts that otherwise may be personally unavailable to them or that go unrecognized and undervalued in the world outside.

To do this, I cannot just talk *about* reading or abstractly describe it, when that is precisely not what I shall claim to be a literary way of thinking. Rather, reading is something that must be done, with immersed attention, inside specific examples. The shared examples offered to the reader throughout this book, to tell its story and make its argument, are neither intentionally polemical nor over-deliberately inclusive but, inevitably, personal choices gathered without plan in the course of a life and triggered by present occasions. That in itself is part of the book's subject matter: how people find for themselves, through their reading, specific deep places for contemplation.

Thinking of the great list in Philippians—whatsoever things are honest, are just, pure, lovely, of good report, think of these things— Iris Murdoch concludes, 'Every individual has a collection of such things.'[2] That personal collection or mental library must also have room here for the things in life that are of pain, mistake, temptation, and difficulty. In short, I include thinking that has arisen out of work I have previously done on Shakespeare, the Victorians, Samuel Johnson, Bernard Malamud, and various aspects of the experience of reading, in an attempt at summation of a reading life.

But for different people, of course, there must be different authors and different books that matter, and different places of emphasis

within them. There is, rightly, a wide variety of literature(s) and
many different views about what literature is: mine is a personal
view, as befits a series that aims to offer a range of such. 'I am what
I am or I am nothing,' says J. H. Newman, 'I cannot think, reflect,
or judge about my being, without starting from the very point which
I aim at concluding.' But, he adds, 'if I do not use myself, I have no
other self to use'.[3]

In what follows, Chapter 1 is an account of how literature offers
its readers what I call a 'holding-ground' for thinking about experience, and what are its characteristics. Chapter 2 goes further into
the experience of what it is like to do careful reading-work within
that arena, with all the extra human potential it offers through a
form of thinking not pre-determined but pitched in the midst of life
between first and last things. Chapter 3 asks what is the relation
between that literary holding-ground and the world itself, in the
exploratory search for meaning. Each chapter begins with an introduction and is divided into sections (three in the first two chapters,
two in the last), with each section sub-divided by headings which are
intended to allow the reader more easily to enter into the literary
examples without loss of the argument. I can't say how many influences, books, and people, have gone into this work, but I am not
ungrateful.

Philip Davis

Liverpool

Notes

1. W. R. Bion, *Learning From Experience* (London: Heinemann, 1962), 84.
2. Iris Murdoch, *Metaphysics as a Guide to Morals* (London: Chatto & Windus, 1992), 335.
3. John Henry Newman, *An Essay in Aid of a Grammar of Assent*, first pub-lished 1870, chapter 9, section 1.

Contents

1

Not Names but Places

Introduction

Wordsworth is a writer who frequently offers the exploratory reader in the midst of life a place from which to start. Trying to find access to his own thoughts, Wordsworth spoke of remembering *how* he felt at a particular time, but *what* exactly he felt he did not recall:

> but that the soul,
> Remembering how she felt, but what she felt
> Remembering not, retains an obscure sense
> Of possible sublimity, to which
> With growing faculties she doth aspire,
> With faculties still growing, feeling still
> That whatsoever point they gain, they yet
> Have something to pursue.
> (*The Prelude* (1805), 2.334–41)

The 'how' that Wordsworth works from here—the obscure, possible, growing feeling of inchoate thoughts—is not merely the how of ornamental literary style, of how most exquisitely to phrase what one already exhaustively knows. It is more like the poet on a walk whom Proust describes—halted for some time by some thought or object, then returning home quickly and silently as though 'afraid of spilling' what he has gathered, before ever he has had the chance to get it into the care of words.[1]

In A. S. Byatt's novel *Still Life* a woman sits in a library, first time away from her recently born baby, reading Wordsworth's 'Immortality Ode' in an attempt to get back some of the thinking-time she took for granted as a single, unencumbered student. She now has a husband, a baby, responsibilities, worries, and little time; yet she says to herself that she must not think about those things for the while but of the 'Immortality Ode' instead. Only then she thinks: all these things—the potential of a baby, the burdens of an adult, the movement of both loss and gain in going from one to the other—*are* what the poem is about. But that does not make it a set of itemized ideas; it makes it a place of refuge in which to find and sift her thoughts. So, connection made again, she reads the poem once more, closer to herself, until suddenly she sees how two quite separate little uses of the word 'deep' silently link and work together in the poem, creating between them again a glimpse of that vision of the power of darkness essential to Wordsworth. What she has done is perhaps nothing much after all, since she soon finds it settle back into a banal and easy insight; but for the time in which it happened it was, indeed, like a moment of vision.

For the attentive reader of Wordsworth or Proust, the 'how' is not to be converted too quickly into the 'what'—the theme or message. Theirs is a language to be examined intently in 'deep', for its reactivated surprises and secrets, as if it were not just a medium of simple external communication but a means of opening and reopening, innerly shifting and deepening, mental pathways. Otherwise, what we all too often have to offer instead are our ready-made opinions and clichéd agendas; the acceptable social attitudes and the habitual stories of one's self that make nothing new.

It is easy enough to spot these formulae in others. There is a recent book by Barbara Ehrenreich called *Smile or Die* which is sub-titled 'How Positive Thinking Fooled America and the World'. In it the author lists the often cruelly coercive assumptions of the life-coaches, the motivational thinkers, and their self-help books in their insistence on thinking positively—and only positively.

The vocabulary is predictable, and it determines the thinking that goes with it. 'To be disappointed, resentful or downcast' is to show yourself to be nothing more than a 'victim', a 'loser', or a 'whiner'. 'If you expect things to get better,' it is urged in the best-selling self-help manuals, 'they will.' After all, in life, we are told, 'we all make choices'. Consequently in the simple pluses and minuses of this accountancy, what is not going your way in life is disposable. So it is with people: 'Get rid of negative people in your life. They waste your time and bring you down. If you can't get rid of them (like a spouse or a boss), reduce your time with them.' As it is with thoughts: 'Whenever a negative thought concerning your personal powers comes to mind, deliberately voice a positive thought to cancel it out.' Accordingly, even as he gave out redundancy-notices, one employer was confidently claiming: 'People do come to see that losing a job was a step forward in their lives.' Herself diagnosed with malignant breast neoplasm, Ehrenreich did not relish the invitation to 'embrace cancer' or the public testimonies of those who had: 'If I had to do it over again, would I want breast cancer? Absolutely. I'm not the same person I was, and I'm glad I'm not.' This is a willed optimism, she concludes, an over-determined expectation, in place of the language of hope. 'Positive thinking' is an ideology in denial of genuine thinking, whereas hope is a vulnerable emotion which knows it is not entirely within its yearner's control, any more than in control of the future.

But the problem is not simply to do with what one can see easily enough in the extremes of others. Rather it is to do with a defective equipment for thinking in oneself, equipment not so flawed, however, that one cannot continue unthinkingly using it. I mean such habits of mind—sustained within an insidiously lazy default language—as trap their owners within the set tracks that precisely avoid the reality of what they think they are talking about.

One of the most frightening accounts of that almost unavoidable and unrecognizable self-blindness is in John Stuart Mill's essay on the philosopher Bentham, his father's mentor in the creation of utilitarianism, the measuring of usefulness. What Bentham proposed was that the utility of all human concerns could be quantified in terms of a simple calculation of the balance of pain and of pleasure in any individual or any number of individuals in society. The principle of 'the greatest happiness of the greatest possible number' was a radical measure of human benefit designed to steer public policy through the confusion of a new industrialized, urban mass society. But when, even in this, Bentham is wrong

it is not because the considerations which he urges are not rational and valid in themselves, but because some more important principle, which he did not perceive, supersedes those considerations. The bad part of his writings is his resolute denial of all that he does not see, of all truths but those which he recognises. ('Bentham', 1838)

This should be the great fear of the thinker who would be comprehensive and systematic: that whatever element is, even unknowingly, omitted or forgotten at the beginning of enquiry will cause the conclusions to fail at the end of it. It is like setting up our rocket on the launch-pad half a degree out of true: once launched we travel on not knowing how far, increasingly, we are lost in space. 'Nobody's synthesis', Mill concludes, 'can be more complete than his analysis.'

But what literature does, which formal philosophy for example commonly does not—and what literature can hardly help doing— is yield more than its writers know. In thinking about human life, it offers as much excess, untidied material as it can by not only thinking but re-creating the very objects of thought—offering more from within the very middle of things, I will argue, than a more secondary discipline can provide with more formally set starts and goals. Writers offer this by creating not so much a line of argument as a resonant space for thinking. In a book on his reading called *A Dish of Orts* (1893), the Victorian fantasy writer George MacDonald speaks of Wordsworth as a poet not so much offering ideas as putting the reader into the *places* (physical, mental, and situational) from which such ideas originally arise so that they come of themselves.[2]

To a literary thinker there is always what Bergson called the invisible 'fringe' of meaning, where fringe signifies all that which darkly surrounded the evolution of a distinct idea, as its origin and its potential.[3] What it comes out of, what it goes towards, still latently and subliminally surrounds that final idea which thoughts become. It is proper that thoughts become consolidated into a shorthand 'idea', something in which mentally to carry them around, for use; but it is not all right when in turn the idea becomes deadened into dry residual opinion. To bring ideas back to life, they need places in which to *be* thought again, places closely approximate to the origin that stimulated them into being, where there is room to maximize that aura or resonance which lies around and behind an idea, so as to be thought and felt again as if for the first time.

But when our thoughts get separated from the memory of the places or occasions or people that first brought them into existence, we become increasingly entrapped in the routine hardening of our mental arteries. There can be an almost automatic default in the assertion of prejudice as principle, in the rapid assumption of those cynical set-attitudes that the novelist Marilynne Robinson, for example, laments: 'When a good man or woman stumbles, we say "I knew it all along", and when a bad one has a gracious moment, we sneer at the hypocrisy.'[4] No serious reader of George Eliot's *Middlemarch* or of Marilynne Robinson's *Home* would automatically think that. There is, similarly, a cautionary occasion in Nadine Gordimer's *The Lying Days*, when a young white South African woman overhears a neglected member of her liberal group say something unusual which is not immediately acceptable to the party line. He simply suggests that to think everything as due to racial prejudice is itself a prejudice. Jolted, she thinks to herself: 'It was a change of focus of the kind that interested me.'

Novels excel in that sort of sudden shift of point of view. Cut off from such revisionary changes of focus when the habitually general suddenly gives way to the new or reclaimed particular, our thoughts only become fixed habits of mind. We resort to what we *think* we think or what we are tacitly persuaded to sign up to. The literal is not the literary. A reading expert, Keith Oatley, reports that scanners show that once a metaphor becomes clichéd it no longer activates the brain's motor system across domains as it did when new; my own collaborators in cognitive science have demonstrated how a dramatically compressed Shakespearean coinage such as 'this old man godded me' excites the brain in a way that 'this old man deified me' or 'made a god of me' does not.[5] Predictable opinions and conventional formulations merely flat-line, going along the boring old mental pathways they thereby reinforce.

We know so little of what actually happens in the act of serious reading. An early twentieth-century researcher, Edmund Huey, travelled the United States investigating the teaching and practice of reading. 'To completely analyse what we do when we read,' he wrote, 'would almost be the acme of a psychologist's achievements, for it would be to describe very many of the most intricate workings of the human mind, as well as to unravel the tangled story of the most remarkable specific performance that civilization has learned in all its history.'[6] In all its youthful mix of limitations, possibilities, and even fantasies, brain-imaging is no more and no less than one (currently fashionable) part of a greater aspiration that must do its exploratory work at various levels and by diverse methods. The aspiration is to find what unrecognized or neglected powers the mind employs, what hidden shapes it takes, in the most powerful personal forms of reading, culminating in the experience of poetic thinking.

What follows in this opening chapter, then, speaks on behalf of a language used for something other than the reductive naming of themes or the delimiting of topics; something more than the paraphrases of opinion or the catch-all nouns of explanation or the strict linearity of argument. In literature, by the creation of felt context and underlying situation, thoughts show where they have come from, what they are related to and summoned by. This involves a writer finding a place, a site, for what otherwise might have no obvious place in the conventional epistemological frameworks of the world.

1. What is a holding-ground?

Creating significant space

Though a literary language is not just about the words, let's start with words, and with one word: only it is a missing word, a word that will not come to mind.

William James, philosopher, psychologist, and brother of the novelist Henry James, was interested when he found himself seeking for a missing word that something in his current situation seemed urgently to call for. That in itself is James's first major point: that words are not learnt or sought for their own sake but in the endeavour of *going after* things, in the process of pursuing them and trying to reach them. 'There is a gap therein,' he writes of this experience of blind mental search for meaning, 'but no mere gap':

It is a gap that is intensely *active*. A sort of wraith of the name is in it, beckoning us in a given direction, making us at moments tingle with the sense of our closeness, and then letting us sink back without the longed for term.[7]

You try this word and it's a lazy cliché; you try another perhaps more elaborate word but still it doesn't seem to fit or catch that 'wraith', that ghost or spirit of meaning intuited, as it were, at the back of the mind. Perhaps someone you know may helpfully suggest a general term that more or less covers what you seem to intend. But if that isn't what you mean inside, you feel yourself as individual to be normalized and stereotyped, and have almost to look away to keep that missing meaning still in mind. Because in all these efforts—

if wrong names are proposed to us, this singularly definite gap acts immediately so as to negate them. They do not fit into its mould. And the gap of one word does not feel like the gap of another, all empty of content as both might seem necessarily to be when described as gaps. (PP i. 251)

It is far from comfortable to be stuck in that vacant but resonant space where you do not know, automatically, what is the next thing to say or write or do, only the wrong ones. But even as it jams the normal process of verbalization, this struggle for articulacy points to an unnamed 'something' creatively important within human beings— a compressed sense of meaning that needs language, is thoroughly imbued with linguistic possibilities, but exists ahead of its own formulation in words. James believed that a good third of our psychic life consists in 'these rapid premonitory perspective views of schemes of thought not yet articulate' (PP i. 253). The struggle to find words is a nascent form of poetry, about knowing and yet not-knowing at different levels. In writing, the not-knowing that goes on in front of the eyes, as they fix on the blank of the page, is trying to get in touch with that silently inchoate knowing that exists just behind them. When the knowing and not-knowing meet, it is an event that seems to make existence whole again.

So here, with Gerard Manley Hopkins fighting his own hopelessness:

> NOT, I'll not, carrion comfort, Despair, not feast on thee;
> Not untwist—slack they may be—these last strands of man
> In me ór, most weary, cry *I can no more.* I can;
> Can something, hope, wish day come, not choose not to be.

The poem is made out of what is almost a stutter of 'not' and 'can'. What is so powerful is the invisible two-way movement in all this: the way in which the poet puts down his monosyllabic starting-points and finds his own words return back upon him as half-thoughts prompting their further formulation. Thus the opening 'Not' builds into 'I'll not', then 'not feast, not untwist'; while the half-stifled cry 'can no more' is heard and met by the return 'I can'. Then it is 'can—*something*' and '*not* choose *not* to be', the poet using whatever he has already got, however incomplete or negative, for more than he usually can. This is language serving as micro-surgery, doing intricate internal work where the normal thick fingers operate too clumsily. But such language must work on the very verge of the inarticulate when recourse to the refuge of easy names and obvious states (the terrible comfort of 'despair') is all too dangerously tempting.

'Namelessness *is* compatible with existence' (PP i. 251), James concludes magnificently. It means that something inarticulate *is* there demandingly in the gap of a missing meaning, and even in its resistance to make-dos, is looking for a further future existence for itself. That anterior stuff—prior to formulation—is precisely what the act of formulation points to and lives off. Without it, we do not start in the right place but too far on, in educated articulateness where words come easy but cheap.

What searching for the right word creates is, at the least, the sense of significant space, a space which it is necessary to fill in the right way, or the wrong way may lose and destroy it. Then if it works a sentence becomes an achievement—as George Henry Lewes, partner to George Eliot, describes when a writer is on the threshold of articulation:

The words float suspended, soulless, mere sounds. No sooner are these floating sounds grasped by the copula, than in that grasp they are grouped into significance: they start into life, as a supersaturated saline solution crystallizes on being touched by a needle-point.[8]

The copula is a word that connects subject and predicate—typically 'is'. This is—what? Can—something. Or three words together, suddenly crystallizing into sense: 'wish day come'. In both senses, the words then 'start' into life.

I wish we could hold on to that sense of the start and the point just before it—that invisible generative place, all too soon absorbed again into the language-process in which it can seem only a means to the end called 'communication'. What is important here is something coming into a language that serves as more than a means: it is the invisible presence of mind behind, within, and between its words. For I think that wraith of meaning exists not only when you cannot find the right word but also after you have found it—in the release of meaning surrounding a verbal breakthrough, the ghost of competing words invisibly surrounding the finally chosen ones.

The example of Wordsworth

In a sonnet 'There is a pleasure in poetic pains', Wordsworth tells of how the thought of writing a 'luckless word', in the midst of composition, often obsessively pursues the poet 'to the social board', 'haunts him belated on the silent plains'. Wordsworth has always been a good place from which to start—the poet most accessible to unpoetical natures, as J. S. Mill called him in his *Autobiography*. Wordsworth knew what it was to be blocked as a writer—the opening 300 lines of *The Prelude* are full of such inner frustration—yet fundamentally trusted that to see a problem was to see something hidden that might yet be accessible.[9]

Imagine, then, if Wordsworth were writing this last stanza to the poem 'She dwelt among the untrodden ways', and had got to the sudden climactic of the penultimate line, looking for the final breakthrough:

> She lived unknown, and few could know
>   When Lucy ceased to be;
> But she is in her grave, and, oh,

—And oh what? This Lucy was a young woman of no ostensible importance in the world; now dead. Suppose that 'oh!' marks the pre-verbal spot where the mental gap was, the threshold across which the words might or might not come to fit the rhymed mould created for them. Suppose (and this is purely my invention[10]) Wordsworth had then tried this, as perhaps most of us might:

>   and, oh,
> The loss it is to me!

But that's not it, says the summoning gap. The poet needs a breakthrough, and a breakthrough is what language should be when it most matters—not the petrified thought that is names and opinions. Wordsworth actually wrote this instead:

> But she is in her grave, and, oh,
> The difference to me!

The *difference* is something that reverberatingly *happens* here, properly filling the space left for it, but also like a deep private blow again to the heart. Private because that felt difference does not take the name of a single emotion such as 'sadness'; it does not name emotion at all. In not saying explicitly what that difference is, and not having to, 'the difference' is thus like a brief and secret epitome of what language most serves for: *it* gives the word, but *you* feel its meaning.

It is like Wordsworth's account of his poem 'Resolution and Independence' in which in the midst of dejection he comes upon an old man: 'A lonely place, a Pond, by which an old man *was*...not stood, not sat, but "*was*".' Words as fundamental as 'the difference' or 'was' were too barely, starkly demanding of meaning, says Coleridge, for those impoverished readers he defined as the enemies of Wordsworth, who needed a more elaborate poetic prompt:

his works make them restless by forcing them in on their own worthless Selves—and they recoil from the Heart, or rather from the place where the Heart ought to be, with a true Horror Vacui.[11]

Unable to give a basic response, they fear the hollowness inside themselves that needs the stimulus of embellishment. They are, writes Wordsworth to Coleridge, people

> who are fed
> By the dead letter, not the spirit of things,
> Whose truth is not a motion or a shape
> Instinct with vital functions, but a block
>   (*The Prelude* (1805), 8.297–9)

The readers for whom Wordsworth was looking instead were those who had sufficient imagination to realize that it is often the minimal and the humdrum, rather than the highest version of a thing, which may be closest to what is fundamental:

In an obscure corner of a Country Church-yard I once espied half-overgrown with Hemlock and Nettles, a very small Stone laid upon the ground, bearing nothing more than the name of the Deceased with the date of birth and death, importing that it was an Infant which had been born one day and died the next.

To Wordsworth that most minimal 'difference' between there being something and there being nothing—just one day of unfulfilled life—is the greatest difference there is. 'A violet by a mossy stone' is how he thought of Lucy, 'half hidden from the eye'. So it is in the churchyard with this barely named Infant who never spoke and barely lived:

I know not how far the Reader may be in sympathy with me, but more awful thoughts of rights conferred, of hopes awakened, of remembrances stealing away or vanishing were imparted to my mind by that Inscription there before my eyes than by any other that it has ever been my lot to meet with upon a Tomb-stone.[12]

Such sympathetic readers are what Wordsworth also called *silent poets* in common life, thinking powerful thoughts amidst ostensibly prosaic sights, without ever writing anything down.

Creating a holding-ground

It is not just bringing a word into being that is William James's concern. Though James talks about these pre-conscious 'gaps' as though summoning the right words to fill themselves, he is even more interested in what he calls the wider 'fields' of human consciousness and how they are established.

Human beings have to be selective, says James, if they are not to be bombarded by the great booming, buzzing confusion of the undifferentiated world. Accordingly, we create narrow fields of consciousness in order to focus and survive. But those fields are only relatively stable, not fixed, just as consciousness itself is not an entity but a changing process. As soon as there lights up in the brain some new force of emotional interest, there is a corresponding shift in the mind's centre of attention and energy, and the field of consciousness around it.

What especially interests James is all that lies at and just beyond the margin of any temporary field of consciousness. By analogy with Faraday's work on electro-magnetism, he speaks of a magnetic field that exists outside and around the narrow focus of consciousness, to which our centre of energy turns like a compass needle. Just outside our immediate ken, an unclassified residuum—floods of memories, masses of residual powers—waits to come in.[13]

James's active sense of gap, blindly pulsating with potential meaning, offers more when taken beyond the search for a single word
and extended into consciousness's investigation of some initially
ill-defined area of human concern lodged somewhere within the
investigator.

Imagine, then, a person who is baffled by his own situation but
needs to inhabit and understand it with all the resources he or she
can muster. The philosopher R. G. Collingwood sketches one such
version:

> At first, he is conscious of having an emotion, but not conscious of what this
> emotion is. All he is conscious of is a perturbation or excitement, which he
> feels going on within him, but of whose nature he is ignorant. While in this
> state, all he can say about his emotion is: 'I feel…I don't know what I feel.'
> From this helpless and oppressed condition he extricates himself by doing
> something.[14]

The something that he or she *does*, says Collingwood, is to make
language—not as simple naming but a language that becomes
exploratory once it has ceased to be automatic. Crucially, such a
person is not one who knows in advance, whatever the intimations
in the back of the mind. For the emotions happen before the
person in whom they occur knows what their name is. Namelessness *is* compatible with existence. And yet in education, from lower
to higher, from continuous professional development to motivational training courses, we insist on 'agreed learning outcomes' set
up in advance, totally planned lessons even in improvisation,
themed structures, constrained syllabi—all for the sake of what are
called 'effective learning behaviours'. It is nothing like the way we
think.

What the baffled person needs to do is to set up a focal space, a
field, which represents the nameless dilemma, in order to create
what we might call a holding-ground for investigation and contemplation. That space could be the map or mould that a sonnet pro-
vides; it could be the recollected landscape in which a poet such as
Wordsworth mentally stakes out his thinking; or simply the area
marked out by a potential story and the interrelationships its premise
involves. In his *Apologie for Poetrie* (1585) Sir Philip Sidney spoke of
'an imaginative groundplot of a profitable invention'.[15]

Certain sonnets

Take Philip Sidney's 'Certain Sonnet 19', beginning 'If I could think how these my thoughts to leave.' It is a poem of rejected love and what then, if anything, to do with the thought of it. In it the poet twists and turns, so that when one line of thought says 'If x', it is always followed by the next line saying 'Or if y', x's opposite, thus going through a range of rhymed alternatives within a sort of poetic thought-machine:

> If I could think how these my thoughts to leave,
> > Or thinking still my thoughts might have good end:
> > If rebel sense would reason's law receive
> > Or reason foil'd would not in vain contend...

The poem's pattern is what I will call a language-within-language— it tacitly says to its reader: Take this line with that one, take every 'If' with its equivalent 'Or', and measure both the symmetries and the differences between them as you read down as well as across the page. The familiar love-story is the ground-plot and the poetic form is the invention. From a third dimension above, the writer's mind can map and trace its own thoughts here, one by one on the two-dimensional page before it, and the reader is expected to follow. The poem's mould thus is made into a holding-ground for thinking thoughts, 'an orb of order and form' as Samuel Daniel called these little poetic worlds.[16] But inside the emotional *dis*order of the content, 'these my thoughts' will not respond to the control of their thinker, his would-be active verbs left ineffectually pre-empted at the end of the lines ('leave', 'receive', 'contend'). One way or another, says the poet tacitly beneath the austere formal elegance: Get me out of this dilemma.

The second quatrain in the next stanza responds to this silent inner cry by taking the linear alternation to a higher level, shifting 'these thoughts' from what 'I' can do in stanza one to what 'you' might do here—and begins again:

> If either you would change your cruel heart
> > Or cruel (still) time did your beauty stain:
> > If from my soul this love would once depart
> > Or for my love some love I might obtain...

The reader is again expected to track the almost computerized movements of this second brain, there on the page, trapped in its own mechanisms. Nothing is ever just for 'once' here, done with for once and all; everything is at least twice over, first one way and then another, again and again. In this way the poem actually *works* within itself: it thinks, its brain has internal synaptic connections, as it were. Thus 'change' in the first line of this second stanza is counterpointed by 'still' in the second line, the two underlyingly interconnected in this mapped-out page-mind by the repeated 'cruel'. '*From* my soul' in the third line is in its desperation similarly played off against '*for* my love' in the fourth, with 'my soul' and 'this love' trying like autonomous parts to get into the right relation between themselves. But if the poem's language-law is that for every 'I' there is a 'you', and for every 'If' an 'Or', then that fourth line should read:

> Or for my love *your* love I might obtain

With quiet devastation there is unannounced *change* in the symmetry of things, a significant variation which shows the situation as suddenly worse. The poet has given up hope of equality: he can't expect 'your love' as part of the ideal machine; instead only, at best, '*some* love'. Suddenly we see why that tiny word 'some' breaks into the little mental world of this poem, though who would have thought that 'some' could be the most emotional and human word in the whole poem? It is not that this poem is nothing but a machine, but that without its machinery it could not be *more* than a machine.

It is, in the words of Elizabeth Barrett Browning in her *Sonnets from the Portuguese*, 'A place to stand and love in for a day | With darkness and the death-hour rounding it' (22): a place to do thinking about disprized love. The Sidney poem ends, breaking down into the very elements out of which it was compounded in the first place:

> I yield and strive, I kiss and curse the pain:
> Thought, reason, sense, time, you, and I, maintaine.

Here it is never simply and naturally 'you and I' together, as in the ordinary speech of 'we'; but 'you, and I' (for this is what the precision of poetry has become) amongst so many other separated things in this world. That comma stands for the relation and the hidden emotion within it that made this have to be a poem: an alternative place, where the relations between the words replace the relationship between the people, in order to sort out in this medium what cannot be sorted out in the other. It is a second life, a model of life, that first must move away from life's feeling to language's form only then to return from that language back to the feeling felt within such a phrase as 'some love'. With such a poem, in all its interconnections, what the writer and the reader have in front of their eyes is a mini-brain.

The example of Shakespearean drama

But a sonnet structure is, at least outwardly, ready-made. There have to be other literary means for trying to create a field which is not as formally closed or self-contained. This requires what I will call the creation of significant space, apt for development. One can see it being formed, as with a single stroke of the brush, in the way, for example, that Coleridge describes Shakespeare as doing in making a creative space for himself to operate within. 'One admirable secret of his art,' writes Coleridge, pointing to the simplest of starting-points:

is that separate speeches frequently do not appear to have been occasioned by those which preceded and which are consequent upon each other, but to have arisen out of the peculiar character of the speaker.[17]

It is not 'What is the news from Rome?' lamely followed by 'I am glad you asked me that. It is this:...' There is no angle of deflection, no extra dimension dynamically created between these two, as there always must be in Shakespeare. To take a classic example, the young man Malcolm immediately urges Macduff to vengeance upon Macbeth following the sudden slaughter of his wife and babes:

> Be comforted:
> Let's make us med'cines of our great revenge,
> To cure this deadly grief.

To which Macduff responds:

> He has no children. (*Macbeth*, 4.3.246–9)

In that reply the abrupt almost inner speech of 'he' may refer to Macbeth ('so how can I really take revenge on him?') but may also be Malcolm himself ('he—I can't even say "you" directly—can't imagine what this loss feels like'). For the Victorian critic John Ruskin this was one of his favourite examples of the rush of what he called 'imagination penetrative'—where in every word, 'often obscure, often half-told' and 'impatient of detailed inter-pretation', there is as though from another suddenly revealed inner dimension 'an awful undercurrent of meaning, and evi-dence and shadow upon it of the deep places out of which it has come'.[18]

What is thus created in this dialogue is not only two distinct points of view but also, thirdly, a sense of the very space *between* them, like a Grecian urn emerging amidst the two facing profiles in the famous illusion:

MALCOLM: Dispute it like a man.
MACDUFF: I shall do so.
But I must also feel it as a man. (4.3.253–5)

That is what it means to create what William James might call a dense and dramatic three-dimensional force-field, with different cen-tres of energy and gravity acting and reacting upon another within it, rather than just a temporal sequence of set-up speeches following on from one another. Or to put it in Wordsworth's terms, this is not just a dead 'block' of material but something that has 'a shape' and a living 'motion' within that shape.

The creation of an energy-field by a writer for the generation of thoughts is what offers both writer and reader a holding-ground for the contemplation of experience.

The example of Hardy's poetry

'Much of life (persons, places, events) does not get turned into knowledge.'[19] But that is what literature can do: make a frame for some area of being that you didn't previously realize could be a subject matter, or, realizing, still did not know how to enter or explore. But when you do enter into it, it is like the magic mirrors or patterned carpets or library doors in the fiction of the Victorian fantasy writer George MacDonald: they let you into a sphere that not only gives room for those lost or latent thoughts to *be* thought but is itself generative of more and more of them.

Here, then, is Thomas Hardy writing of the ostensibly simple experience of being stood up, in the formal frame of the poem 'A Broken Appointment':

> You did not come,
> And marching Time drew on, and wore me numb.—
> Yet less for loss of your dear presence there
> Than that I thus found lacking in your make
> That high compassion which can overbear
> Reluctance for pure lovingkindness' sake
> Grieved I, when, as the hope-hour stroked its sum,
>   You did not come.
>
> You love not me,
> And love alone can lend you loyalty;
> —I know and knew it. But, unto the store
> Of human deeds divine in all but name,
> Was it not worth a little hour or more
> To add yet this: Once, you, a woman, came
> To soothe a time-torn man; even though it be
>   You love not me?

The first stanza begins with the bare line and the stark fact, 'You did not come', and ends with it, as though unable to get over it. Likewise, symmetrically the second stanza begins with 'You love not me' and ends on it, albeit with a question mark that desperately seeks room, even at the end, to hope against hope. But what is most powerful is when the reader no longer takes the stanzas as two separately statically rhymed 'blocks' but suddenly sees the gap come to life between them

> You did not come.
>
> You love not me.

—which William James might call a gap made meaningfully active. There is no moment when someone *not* turning up actually *happens*: instead, the meaning sinks in and has to be inferred in that time-made-into-space between the end of the first and the beginning of the second stanza. That inter-stanza space then comes forward like something no longer subordinate but alive in its own right, wherein one can feel and almost see the inner processes of hurt realization sinking in. What is more, 'You love not me' is in part a *consequence* of that hurt interval between the stanzas but also, at the moment it is written, the *creator* of it as well, retrospectively, just behind itself. In that momentary see-saw between movements forward and back, this is the definitively human mixture of the active and the passive as it goes into the act of writing. And for once, in this poem, that resonant store of meaning within which the work takes place, and which the work has also helped to create and extend, is made *visible* in the blank, silent, and yet charged space that comes to exist between 'You did not come' and 'You love not me'.

That space is an image of literature's holding-ground: it holds the inner meaning, just as certain places in Hardy's Wessex seemed to hold the memory of what passed for him there. For Hardy at such points, to employ the words of Wordsworth, 'the hiding places of my power | Seem open'.[20] Then it is as though his poem almost looks back at him even as he writes it. For Hardy is his own best reader for being vulnerable to his own words in the very act of writing. He puts himself into his poetry, and then finds his own poetry coming back at him, almost speaking back to him. It is as if—and this is crucial—the page had become a *second* version of his own mind transferred now into the poem. Then when Hardy sees what he has just written, he can often hardly bear the sight of the lines. 'You love not me?' Or, just before another long-awaited meeting, Hardy finds himself:

> ... knowing that what is now about to be
> Will all *have been* in O, so short a space!
> > ('The Minute before Meeting')

The italics are his own: even as time goes past in relatively slow motion—'what is now/what-is-now about-to-be/to-be Will-*have-been*'— the sight and the inner meaning of his own words hurts him again.

In the third chapter of *The Return of the Native* (1878), Hardy writes, 'People with any weight of character carry, like planets, their atmospheres along with them in their orbits.' But I am saying that this is true not only of some persons but of experiences and thoughts and words themselves. It is just that such forces need something approximating to their proper place in which truly to be thought about and not just paraphrased; in which their surrounding nimbus, aura, resonance, feel, or atmosphere can be recalled and realized as a dimension of the meaning.

It becomes worse in a baffling situation when you think you know what you 'should' be feeling but whatever it is doesn't seem quite to fit the prescribed names. Hardy himself would know what the bereaved protagonist of Clive Sinclair's *A Soap Opera from Hell* (1998) meant, when in his loss he finds

he can readily describe the externals, but lacks a vocabulary to explain his feelings. No. The vocabulary exists. What is missing is an internal dictionary to provide individual meanings. He is familiar with the word 'grief', but cannot be sure he has experienced it.

Hardy was unhappily married for years, but when Emma Hardy died and he read the early happy love-letters she kept and the personal diary she wrote in later years, he was devastated. Ordinary solid language won't serve at such a point: as though separately, there could be sorrow, guilt, surprised loneliness, regret, bereavement, depression. What Hardy seeks, within the external vocabulary of mere naming, is an *internal* dictionary—a language-within-language—to provide individual meanings too deep, subtle, and interrelated for simple common nouns.

So in search of the right space in which to think about his wife, Hardy stands in their garden where she used to tend the flowers. Later he stands there again in his writing, in 'The Shadow on the Stone': there he thinks he sees the shadow of his dead wife cast a foot or two in front of him, as if she were just behind his shoulder. Here are the second and third stanzas of the poem:

> And I said: 'I am sure you are standing behind me,
>   Though how do you get into this old track?'
>   And there was no sound but the fall of a leaf
>   As a sad response; and to keep down grief
> I would not turn my head to discover
>   That there was nothing in my belief.
>
>   Yet I wanted to look and see
>   That nobody stood at the back of me;
> But I thought once more: 'Nay, I'll not unvision
>   A shape which, somehow, there may be.'

Again in that inter-space between the end of one stanza and the beginning of the next, there is a silent internal language—what I call a poem's language-within-language, tacitly signalled through the deployment of rhymed space and in the counterpoint of line played off against sentence. For again a reader can almost literally see the silent aftermath of that thought 'there was nothing in my belief'. After the end of stanza two (the first stanza above), there indeed *was* and *is* that blank nothing and the challenge of what to do about it.

This wasn't a thought Hardy wanted to think—that there was nothing to it but psychological delusion. The last line of that stanza does what its preceding line did not want it to—namely, 'dis-cover' the absence he must now forever live with:

> and to keep down grief
> I would not turn my head to discover
> That there was nothing in my belief.
>
> Yet I wanted to look and see

Now in the thick of his writing, Hardy can feel the poem speaking back to him—in the cold lineal stare of 'there was nothing in my belief'—even as his dead wife did not. It is as though the poem itself then demands his response, in order to be able to move from one stanza to the next. To attempt that movement in keeping the poem's space alive, Hardy first wrote in his draft for stanza three 'Yet I *felt I must* look and see', before changing it to 'Yet I *wanted* to look and see'. It is like William James, trying for a fit between word and gap. But somewhere even before that, at the back of his mind, he must have also changed his lost original desire: 'I wanted to look and see | That *she*, that *some-body*, stood at the back of me'. Only, it is now 'I wanted to look and see | That *nobody* stood at the back of me', as if hope is almost more emotionally intolerable than disappointment might be. He has become a man stranded between not wanting to know the truth and being unable to bear not to. His only way out is the equivalent double negative of 'not *un*vision', together with 'may' and 'somehow'. It is as though the wish-to-believe is consciously and honourably more substantial than the belief itself. In such twists and turns, Hardy was a greater man than he could almost bear to be.

For Hardy this vulnerable recourse to writing comes out of something the poem itself points to—his speaking directly out loud but then hearing nothing in reply:

And I said, 'I am sure you are standing behind me...'

He still says 'you' not 'she', where 'she' would be the past tense that would extinguish the aura of 'you'. And the reader can almost see the bereaved man standing vulnerably at the end of that line, already hearing the silence in response. For this is a man more aware of himself as 'me', of being looked upon from behind himself, rather than the 'I' who speaks forth:

> And there was no sound but the fall of a leaf
> As a sad response

That is where the writing of this poetry begins, in the failure of speaking and in memory of that failed speaking. Such poetry is then internal speech, transferred from without to within, making within itself a place—like Hardy's space between stanzas—full of tacit feelings, unspoken thoughts, and magnetic inner connections. Literature is that alternative place in which the writer creates openings, 'heaving into uncreated space' as D. H. Lawrence put it in his 'Study of Thomas Hardy'—each significant move of thought not only going on within that poetic space but further sustaining and extending its dominion.[21] This makes for a field both extra-dense and extra-porous compared to the normal fields of consciousness, with sufficient forces within it both to draw in and be pulled towards all that lies beyond the usual threshold of experience. Emotion is vital to that magnetic power; its lit-up and irradiating presence is a message to writer and reader alike, saying: this matters more than you ever quite know.

Visions of the holding-ground

Only the imaginative help of a literary work can truly 'explain' what goes on in the energy-field and holding-ground that literature can constitute.

In Russell Hoban's novel *Fremder*, set in 2052, the protagonist is a flicker-pilot: a man who can be transported from one planet to another almost instantaneously, his molecular structure broken down at one place to be reassembled in the flicker of an instant at his destination. What begins to obsess Fremder, after too many journeys and a trauma during his last one, is the flicker of underlying blackness, the unknowable gap that lies hidden deep in between the disappearance and the reappearance. Within the sub-atomic, micro-second flicker of reality lies the possibility, every time, that this time he might not be re-created. Or even if re-created, the belief in this reappearing self being the same as the one that disappeared comes to seem to him no more than an uncheckable assumption. Forever uncheckable, because to test the apparently solid continuity of being, he would need to see into the first self and the second version, whilst also being a third able to do that seeing.

He has to turn instead to a super brain-imaging machine of 2052, in which he can see the changing shapes and motions of his brain, unsure which is more 'me': the one depicted on the screen or the one who sees it. Here, it is not the case of first thinking something and then watching the brain follow. On the contrary, head-spin-ningly, the thoughts of the seer themselves seem almost anticipated by distinct waves of excited activity which he can register on the monitor. Like Hardy, Fremder is a man who would like to think that he is simply either *here* or *there*, but between the two he hardly knows where he really is.

Thus, as the wired-up Fremder thinks of the idea of flicker, in denial of the too easy idea of a seamless continuity day after day, he feels the particles of his self move apart a little letting in the dark, while the screen-print of his brain assumes within it strange shapes and changing colours and sounds. He needs that screen because without it he cannot catch what is going on in the interstices of the normal reality-envelope, as he calls it. It holds something for him. In it he can see the saturated whirl and shift of his emotions, the imagi-nably raw state he is in, restored to a biological condition before and without words. And when he asks the super-computer what the vibrating purple-blue, like a scream in his eye, stands for—what it is truly that is disturbing him—then 'Terror' is the word thrown up in reply. It is not in this context a mere name: it is almost shriekingly precipitated out of the very space of its existence as the translated culmination of its reality. The word is an event of truth: it is not just 'fear' but a word he has been feeling without wholly knowing it for some long time: Terror, 'older than evolution', 'the oldest thing there is' in deep relation therefore to the black cosmic origin of things.[22]

William James, as a psychologist, might have loved to have seen that pulsar-like gap of his, like a little inner mind, repeatedly seeking a missing word or vital phrase; might have relished the sight on Fremder's super-computer of what he called the hot spots which he felt lit up in the brain when a thought suddenly seemed to come to life. That is what the brain-imaging experiments devised in my own research centre were designed to suggest: poetic lines acting as brain waves, providing a model that would lock into and then modify existing mental pathways.[23] For just as the practice of reading aloud may be educated by the sight of a reader's instinctive choices as registered in a spectrographic print-out of a recording; so the idea that silent readers might see something of the internal motions they intuitively feel inside themselves seems to offer another possible stage in learning. The registering of such movements in the neural system, just below the level of habitual mental categorization—the excited sense of cognitive matter happening speedily and almost physically *before* cognition can take place: these seem to point to deep pre-articulate sources of excited feeling not exhausted by any subsequent ratiocination and worthy of being an acknowledged part of our experience.

Brain-imaging is fashionable, for reasons both good and bad. Arguably good, if popular curiosity comes out of the need to believe again in the existence of a complex inner life, by finding a new language for the understanding of its reality. Not so good perhaps, when the need for the apparently verifying support of science arises out of the felt weakness of the humanities, under threat as mere luxury or soft irrelevance. Literature will go disregarded as a deep form of thinking if only visible and material evidence can seem sufficient against post-humanist scepticism.

Yet if neuroscience is fashionable, slow, deep, literary reading is not. And yet Fremder's imagined screen, copyright 2052, is no more and no less than what the old poems and old fictions used to be and used to do. What lies flickering in the dense interstices of things is what a Thomas Hardy found between stanzas. Literature is *already* a kind of brain-imaging, as the mind looks at verbal versions of the micro-movements of thought inside itself. It is what we saw happening in Sidney's 'If I could think'.

A writer may start with what look like mere blocks on a screen, situational outlines on a page, but they do not stay like that. In *The Marriages Between Zones Three, Four, and Five* (1980), for example, Doris Lessing begins with a liberal, enlightened, and feminized realm called Zone Three, which nonetheless has become infertile and in decline. The mysterious overseers of all the zones, called the Providers, insist that the only cure is for the Queen of that Zone to go down into the inferior and more primitively brutal Zone Four, which is also ailing, to marry its King. On the face of it, this looks like a feminist allegory, the representative of Zone Three, Al-Ith, civilizing the warlike patriarch of Zone Four, Ben Ata. In the novel itself, however, as by a shift of genre, what happens becomes something more humanly complex and two-way: in a sudden change of scale and focus, horizontally across the zones, it becomes a *marriage*; there is a charged relationship between the woman and the man as individually challenging in its to-and-fro between them as anything in D. H. Lawrence. As a result, the zones are no longer discrete blocks of land, for the boundaries between them are no longer closed off but open, as though Zone Four needs a more reflective tenderness in the same way as Zone Three has forgotten some fundamentally necessary toughness.

What is more, there are other changes in the dimensions of this visionary world. When, at the inexplicable demand of the Providers, Al-Ith has to leave her husband in Zone Four and go back to Zone Three, she feels she now carries something of Zone Four within her, as though it were no longer safely geographical but a state of being itself innerly created by the marriage.

Similarly, Ben Alta is instructed by the Providers to go down into Zone Five, and there marry the even more warlike Queen of that realm. At this point, Ben Ata finds himself feeling as he imagines Al-Ith must have felt when, analogously, she was sent down to him, and by that very token realizes he is taking something of her and what she represents into Zone Five.

Meanwhile, Al-Ith finds herself no longer at home in Zone Three which now can revive without her. Her only alternative is to struggle to get into the almost unimaginably far distant world of Zone Two, the higher realm of being to which she is forced to aspire precisely through having descended to Zone Four.

I do no more than sketch here what in the novel itself becomes far more than a sketch-map. But it is a bare image, even so, of two ideas I hope to have consolidated in this section.

The first is the literary use of a situated place, and movement within that place, in order to think in more dimensions than those of flat opinion or common argument—about which I hope sufficient has been said in this section. But the second is to do with the poet, Hardy or Sidney, looking at his own poem in the act of making it, with Fremder staring at his brain-image, and in particular with Ben Ata seeing himself as though through Al-Ith's eyes. As Doris Lessing knows, these acts of self-reflection make for a new stage within the evolution of the human apparatus. It is what the critic Joseph Gold says that literature itself has become for both writers and readers: 'a brain extension', which has added a new level of consciousness to human brains 'because by means of writing and reading the brain could feedback thought to itself'.[24] A *second self* is created by the very act of looking at oneself, or some imagined version of oneself. For that which does the seeing is by that very act necessarily distinct from that which is being seen, without the two being either wholly separate from, or completely the same as, each other. That second self is a vital extra level of recursively created being, making for what the philosopher Hannah Arendt calls the 'two-in-oneness' of a thinker.[25] To Arendt's beloved Socrates, any person who is self-damaged by some sin or trauma has shattered the internal harmony necessary to calm and steady thinking, and almost destroyed the capacity to think of oneself. But what wrecks a calm philosophy creates a powerful literature: the page like another extra brain gives the steadiness which the mind on its own cannot sustain; the poetry gives by its nature a purer clearness of admittance even to what is painfully soiled in content.

Most of us cannot become formal thinkers, as philosophers are trained to be, and our personal subject matter is more informal or inchoate anyway. But for those who wish to use thinking to get above themselves whilst *still* remaining within themselves, it is reading that serves as the trigger for such reflection and as a space for such contemplation. We need the activation of these second selves, or second lives and levels, both on the page and in our minds when reading it.

2. The shape of thoughts

Resonance and syntax—J. H. Newman

Like planets, said Hardy, people who are deep carry their own 'atmosphere' along with them in their movement.

In an unpublished paper of 1868, John Henry Newman imagines a reader who is particularly drawn into the orbit created by the intellectual world of Aristotle. This is not just knowledge at the level of the philosopher's explicit ideas about this or that topic, but an implicit understanding of what may be called the overall weight and feel of the work as a whole, as if it were indeed an integrated living person. Such a reader could almost be Aristotle, or at least be a means of having an Aristotle by proxy for modern times. Yet even such a reader can no more have every thought of Aristotle's explicitly before his mind, says Newman, than could Aristotle himself:

The philosophy, as a system, is stored in the *memory*...and is brought out according to the occasion. A learned Aristotelian is one who can answer any whatever philosophical questions in the way that Aristotle would have answered them. If they are questions which could not occur in Aristotle's age, he still answers them.... In one respect he knows more than Aristotle; because, in new emergencies after the time of Aristotle, he can and *does* answer what Aristotle would have answered, but for the want of opportunity did not.[26]

Of course it is perfectly possible that such a person could be wrong or deluded, distorting the original. And it is an equally obvious objection that Aristotle's thinking, whether a whole or not, is not necessarily applicable to a situation taking place within a quite different historical context. But, on the first count, the most *interesting* thinking goes on at that borderline where one can never be quite sure of the difference between *your* Aristotle and Aristotle *himself*: that is to say, when you are so *full* of your reading of Aristotle that if you cannot wholly and confidently equate the two, you cannot with certainty separate them either. Secondly, reading may indeed be tutored by history and cautioned by historical difference, but still it must risk defying historical limitation when it feels a resonance or excitement, as though the thought needs to be found again and have place again in this present world.

It is this bursting-out or breaking-through of thought—thought from the past that may seem out of season and yet has become resonantly present—that interests me as a form of sudden recognition, obscurely demanding its place of relevance, despite all current agendas. Newman employs a distinction between implicit and explicit thinking for a better understanding of such experiences. If no one can keep all his thoughts explicitly present before him all the time, then there has to be a tacit store, an implicit fullness, so Newman calls it, from which thoughts are elicited into explicitness according to a prompting occasion. That tacit store, like a dynamic memory, is what I have called the *resonance*, or as Hardy says the atmosphere, that the mind carries with and within itself.

Thus when Aristotelians finds themselves in a dilemma not specifically addressed by Aristotle himself, it is as though they bring that *memory* of Aristotle into the space or gap confronting them as both challenge and opportunity. This isn't a matter of merely trying doggedly to 'remember' what Aristotle said, literally and explicitly: when Newman speaks of 'memory meeting occasion' here, he is thinking of a living memory, something old spontaneously coming back to life to meet its occasions in a new shape modified by the current force of surrounding circumstance. 'Principles require a very various application according as persons and circumstances vary, and must be thrown into new shapes according to the form of the society which they are to influence' (*Development*, 58). It is those 'new shapes' that are crucial.

For it is not Aristotle or the Aristotelian specialist as such who interests me. It is anyone making or finding in the world a place for him- or herself, for what they have in them from whatever sources and influences. In particular, I have been talking about people locating a subject-space in which they might more properly think their thoughts than in the norms of life: a resonant field or holding-ground rich enough to make the thoughts part of an activated experience and a three-dimensional situation, without the demand for simple consistency. Writers may create such a place; readers may re-occupy such a place: the point is finding the resonant place and then trying to work within it.

But when a writer does find the opening for such a space, the task is then to occupy it verbally, to hold and extend it, to stay in it and as it were work the field. That is where beside resonance a second term—*syntax*—comes in, in the second place, to do work in realization of that experience of being thrown into new shapes. Syntax is what feels out, and seeks to fill in, those intuited and imagined shapes. It tries to give them visible habitation on the page through the act of sentence-construction. Thus, syntax for Newman is the development of explicit reasoning, in working a field of thought which is occupied, first of all, by the latent and implicit. It is what some now might call the working out of the intuitions of the right hemisphere within the rational action of the left.[27]

Writing, says Newman, 'is the representation of an idea in a medium *not native* to it'.[28] He is insistent that words do not have an easy or literal 1:1 relation to the thoughts they seek to represent; that, likewise, thoughts, being immaterial, are not coterminous with the material beginnings or endings of the sentences in which they have to be lodged. No sentence is ever as fully explicit and self-standing as it may seem, for sentences have to divide meaning between them in order to conquer. Even as writers raised their pen between one sentence and another, there was always implicit, underlying thinking going on before, within, and after each separate unit. Sentences have to be (more-than-literally) *read*: that is to say, tracked down, worked out, and imagined in the process.

Nor does the size of a thought have a direct proportion to the number of sentences that have to be used in order to articulate it. Readers and writers alike have to know how an important idea, suddenly made explicit, could be lost in a tiny sentence; and would have then to be re-won by the remedial syntax of a following sentence. Though seemingly successive, each of the sentences that then follows may still, in invisible mental reality, only be *contained within* the originating sentence that had the great idea implicitly enfolded within it. So it is, say, in D. H. Lawrence's technique of coming again and again at an apprehension of meaning, nearer and nearer, never quite a repetition. Thoughts in such minds struggle to come to themselves, struggle to find the right place for themselves.

But some thoughts, says Newman, simply look odd when made explicit and discrete on the page—cold, abrupt, 'the representation seems out of shape and strange' (*University Sermons*, 270). A syntax has to suggest, signal, shape out, and trigger that sense of the difference between page and mind, back *on* the page itself. For example, this is a brief Newman sentence in defence of the reality of unconscious thinking: 'It is no proof that persons are not possessed, because they are not conscious, of an idea' (*University Sermons*, 321). People can have ideas without being conscious of them, he might have said more simply and assertively. But Newman wants those three negatives ('no', 'not', 'not') in order to show the risk and the difficulty of imagining from this side of consciousness another side of hidden possibility; wants 'possessed' and 'conscious' to run parallel with each other precisely because they are *not* the same thing. He called this complication 'saying and unsaying to a positive result'.[29] The re-writing, the qualifying and refining, remind the reader that there is a writer here having to intervene upon previous statements as a basis for further approximations—and that that human intervention in the struggle for meaning is what writing and what reading are about. 'In other words,' writes Newman, trying again, 'all men have a reason, but not all men can give a reason' (*University Sermons*, 259), the parallel words 'have' and 'give' enlivened by being attracted together though their very distinction. They say in their compressed order: if you cannot immediately *give* the reason why you think x or believe y, that does not mean that the thought and the belief are inherently irrational and should not have been *had* in the first place. Explicit reason for Newman naturally comes in the second place. In risk and in trust, implicit acts of thought come first, their working out only in the sentences that try to follow.

To the literal mind thoughts may seem as separate as the sentences that convey them. But apparently separate propositions, says Newman, 'are ever formed in and round the idea itself (so to speak), and are in fact one and all only aspects of it' (*University Sermons*, 334). It is impossible to convey three or four differing thoughts all at once, even though they may branch out of the same source: only syntax can help to hold together, and even in that distinguish, thoughts which the mind can barely combine on its own. It would have been less of a holding-achievement of mind had Newman written more simply in two separate sentences, 'People may not be conscious of ideas. But they can have them without knowing it', or in their two separate phases 'People have a reason. They cannot always give it.' But his massy syntax helps create the mind that can hold its own thoughts most powerfully together.

All this means that for Newman reading is not in its deepest nature an automatic literal process but one always closer to the metaphoric, *even* in the reading of sentences that are not fiction or verse: to be truly understanding, it implicitly requires an act of interpretation or translation.

Given the creation of a resonant subject-space discussed in section 1, this section aims to examine how, within sentences, syntax explores that space, opens it out, and develops its contours, fashioning those very shapes of thinking that readers follow in their journeying. But as Newman helps recognize, non-fictional prose is a medium of discourse, ostensibly without exceptional advantages and possessed of a merely horizontal ongoingness, which may provide a quasi-basic test of the struggle of serious writing to think in the world. Offering the challenge of fewer formal signals of a language-within-language than does poetry, with its added syntax of lineation and its rhythmic patternings down the lines as well as along them; manifesting nonetheless the need for what we might too narrowly think of as literary qualities of vocabulary and syntax within what we might now suppose to be non-literary genres; it is this sort of prose previously called 'letters'—and the development of a creative syntax in its working out—which is the object of concentration for the remainder of this section.

The example of Johnsonian syntax

Samuel Johnson is the master of the complex periodic sentence, its great re-creator and representative. Vitally different from the basic nuclear sentence, where noun simply meets verb and then object, it is also quite distinct from the loose and open style of narrative where one sentence may simply follow another horizontally in time without an end in view. Combining a number of distinct thoughts in a number of balanced clauses, signalling its course through the use of particles and conjunctions acting as markers and signposts, the classical periodic sentence, as we shall shortly see, is not mentally complete until it discloses its meaningfully integrative end. It was the instrument Johnson relied upon to find his way through his thoughts.

For that reason, he habitually employed in his writing the classic apparatus of clausal symmetries and balanced phrases beloved of the eighteenth century, in its search for a mental mean between extremes. Johnson in this was not unlike Newman's Aristotelian, bringing the general structures of his thought to bear upon the challenge of any particular problem or occasion. But often, in the face of difficulties that will not conform to pre-determined shape, what Johnson actually has to do in practice is turn the symmetrical structures *against* themselves. So it is in the following excerpt in which Johnson considers the Stoic scheme of avoiding emotional pain by practising apathy or indifference in the face of life:

If by excluding joy we could shut out grief, the scheme would deserve very serious attention; but since however we may debar ourselves from happiness, misery will find its way at many inlets and the assaults of pain will force our regard, though we may withhold it from the invitations of pleasure, we may surely endeavour to raise life above the middle point of apathy at one time, since it will necessarily sink below it at another. (*Rambler* 47)[30]

'If could...but since however will...though may...may surely above...since necessarily below': this is syntax working life's complex way as through the eye of a needle. What is telegraphed here is not an easy or even balance, or a fair deal: abstaining from *joy* does *not* prevent *grief*; excluding *happiness* does *not* shut out *misery*; preventing *pleasure* still does *not* cut out *pain*—for even though the failure of all the good feelings may cause a corresponding increase in all the painful ones, still pain, grief, and misery *will* always come anyhow. This could be pessimism but is pessimism innerly transformed, turned back to front, into a motive for courage and risk in the appetite for life. Where no secure middle point is possible, the only counter-balance to life's inevitable downs is the commitment to continue to risk seeking, all the more, its still possible ups. Johnson employs a visibly formal syntax precisely to show how life still eludes a complete formal ordering of itself. The very shape of the writing—what invisibly stops it saying one thing or prevents it turning another way or insists upon another addition—creates by default the inference of all that defeats or defies a simpler mental organization.

That is how that great admirer of Johnson, Samuel Beckett, is in his own way Johnsonian, when he reads Augustine writing on the two thieves crucified beside Christ, one on the right hand, the other on the left:

I am interested in the shape of ideas, even if I do not believe in them. There is a wonderful sentence in Augustine: I wish I could remember the Latin. It is even finer in Latin than in English. 'Do not despair; one of the thieves was saved. Do not presume, one of the thieves was damned.' That sentence has a wonderful shape.[31]

That is the great thought: that ideas have a *shape* in which they are thought, by which they must be lived. When those two phrases—'Do not despair... Do not presume'—sink into the mind like two different centres of gravity, then the reader who wonders how to live between them is fully involved in what may be called the psychology of grammar. The sentencing serves definitely to mark out the indefinite and invisible place between hope and fear in which a life has still to go on. In such unclear but vital spaces, a tough-mindedness is required which, for the reader as time-traveller, may be best represented by what the eighteenth century can offer the human mind.

For all his massive intelligence, there is at the heart of Johnson a conscious feeling of failure, the failure of knowledge to find a clear solution to life. What Johnson's syntax does instead is to demarcate the space within which life has to carry on, even with less than enough. Perhaps his greatest single sentence is this, then, on the subject of not letting fear take over:

Evil is uncertain in the same degree as good, and for the reason that we ought not to hope too securely, we ought not to fear with too much dejection. (*Rambler* 29)

The shape is not merely a style, unless it is the style of the man himself working within the shape made by belief struggling amidst reality. Between those negatives 'not to hope too...' and 'not to fear too...', with no simple middle path, the very arena in which life has to be lived is here inferred and shaped out by his syntax. It is not just the great nouns 'hope' and 'fear' that matter, however substantial they feel in Johnson's hands; nor is it even the opposition between them. Every bit as crucial is the fact that evil is uncertain *'in the same degree'* as good is. So, *'for the reason'* that we should not hope too securely, we should not fear too dejectedly either. That is to say in this language-within-language: both hope and fear are fallible for the *same* reason and to the *same* degree—as part of the same sentence and of the self-same structure of life. This enjoins acceptance, even though we don't know '*the* reason'; only that there is *a* reason that makes it as it is. For what Johnson is about is syntax strenuously worked out from within the very midst of the world, instead of a series of separate feelings or attitudes. There aren't just the basic named feelings of simple anger, love, or joy, says William James: in the evolution of complex combinations of emotion amidst the complex difficulties of existence, there is also an otherwise undefinable feeling of *and*, of *if*, of *but* (PP i. 245, chapter 9). Such syntax can help make thoughts begin to form and re-form a mind capable of thinking them concurrently, can make the mind enable itself to become what has to think those tough thoughts together.

As Saul Bellow's Herzog writes in a half-maddened letter to one of his favourite dead philosophers, Spinoza: 'Thoughts not causally connected were said by you to cause pain. I find that is indeed the case.'[32] Johnson knew equivalent pain in sensing mental gaps and vacuities, in experiencing contradiction and doubt or suffering passivity. Syntax responds to the need, which Bion describes at the opening of this book, to create an apparatus of thinking that can have and bear the thoughts; but the thoughts themselves come first, even though inchoate, and often emotionally thick and fast and unconnected.

Johnson, I suspect, would actually have preferred a full and direct simplicity rather than a complex grammar. There was a rough, almost physical straightforwardness in the man's essence. As Johnson put it to Mrs Thrale in a letter of 27 October 1777, more needily than usual, there is in writing a letter, to a friend, the nearest proximity to his ideal of simplicity and sincerity, without doubt or distrust, where 'everything is said as it is thought':

In a Man's Letters, you know, Madam, his soul lies naked, his letters are only the mirror of his breast, whatever passes within him is shown undisguised in its natural process. Nothing is inverted, nothing distorted, you see systems in their elements, you discover actions in their motives.[33]

The essays in *The Rambler* sought to offer wisdom for the purpose of living well: they had a direct motive, and at some level Johnson would have loved to have written or indeed spoken directly, without the need for defence, qualification, or art. In the ideal of personal letter-writing between friends of congenial minds, he concludes, 'The original Idea is laid down in its simple purity'—ahead of any supervenient conceptions and qualifications that may need to come after.

Yet this naked simplicity cannot be so in his formal public and general writings, in which first principles and clear originals have to be tested, modified, and reshaped amidst the very thick of the fallen world. 'Metaphysical rights entering into common life,' said that great disciple of the school of Johnson, Edmund Burke:

> like rays of light which pierce into a dense medium, are, by the laws of nature, refracted from their straight line.... The primitive rights of men undergo such a variety of refractions, that it becomes absurd to talk of them as if they continued in the simplicity of the original direction.[34]

For the rights of men, Burke concludes, 'are in a sort of middle, incapable of definition, but not impossible to be discerned' (*Reflections*, 152–3). In the same way, Johnson's sentences are themselves not straight lines but have to work their way to understanding through refractions, in the middle of life.

But still a reader senses behind the complex formulations of Johnson 'systems in their elements', 'actions in their motives', 'the original Idea in its simple purity'. What Johnson wrote was: 'for the reason that we ought not to hope too securely, we ought not to fear with too much dejection'; but equally, he could have written 'for the reason that we ought not to fear with too much dejection, we ought not to hope too securely' and yet chose not to. He cannot simply, crudely say: HOPE! But that language-within-language, the hidden choice and difference which the human can make in putting things one way round rather than another, results in Johnson tipping the balance in favour of hope over fear or dejection. That is one of his elements, his motives, his original ideas: when all is equal, to add weight to what can be done, not to what cannot. That is his demarcation: 'It is our duty, while we continue in this complicated state, to regulate one part of our composition by some regard to the other' (*Rambler* 17).

A writer, says Johnson, too often proposes his schemes of life 'in abstraction and disengagement, exempt from the enticements of hope, the solicitations of affection, the importunities of appetite, or the depressions of fear' (*Rambler* 14). Johnson is no such writer. His abstractions lie only in the massy weight of a writing whose general language serves simultaneously to trigger *and* to repress the individual private and personal memories it generically represents. It is as though, on the other side of these powerfully re-doubled phrases, the reader almost physically feels what it was like when, on some particular past occasion, hope did entice or affection did solicit, when appetite importuned, or fear depressed, almost spelling it out within the language's private inner resonances. 'Men more frequently require to be reminded than informed' (*Rambler* 2).

A second or under-language

Literature's language-within-language is formal and sophisticated, and I shall have more to say of it in Chapter 2. But for the moment what I want to add is that what it triggers in the reader is almost its asymmetrical opposite: a colloquial inner voice, a *second language* that is informally more crude, more like the immediate physical emotion of a shorthand, a coded message electrifying de-coded. It says beneath the formal discourse and mingled with one's own voice, in an inner silent roar: HOPE—though I know hope is difficult and dangerous; it says, like a cliché turned near-violent: REMEMBER—and specifically, remember what this means in you. It is triggered thoughts that a reader gets from inhabiting this resonant territory, thoughts internally blurted by a voice not quite out loud.

This telegraphese as we may also call it includes for me (though we seldom tell these tales and perhaps least of all in conventional professional settings) the associated memory of the teacher who introduced me to Johnson and to Hardy. He was a novelist, now dead, and wrote this of one of his old, cultured types:

Alistair cleared plate, coffee cup and percolator, but before he set out for the butcher's shop sat down at the piano to play Haydn. He chose a C major sonata, rippled through the allegro, but suddenly in the second half of the Adagio found himself moved, so that he held his breath while his eyes pricked with tears. Here Haydn touched romanticism, cried for the unattainable, but shortly, with a neat brevity that seemed to deny the power of the feeling encaged in a few bars.[35]

It is the formal eighteenth-century restraint on the one side that almost paradoxically creates the released feeling on the other, like some electrical leap across differing circuits. Stanley Middleton's ageing protagonist is a recently made widower, a retired director of a Midlands education authority, who feels cut off from the land of the living, settling to the piano or some laid-aside book until the world comes back to him a little. He is provincial, not urbane or global, but as Thomas Hardy put it in response to the cultured criticisms of Matthew Arnold: 'A certain provincialism of feeling is invaluable. It is of the essence of individuality, and is largely made up of that crude enthusiasm without which no great thoughts are thought, no great deeds done.'[36] Thus in his nondescript house Alistair will remember or read something—such as a poem about Simon Magus finding Helen of Troy a housewife in Antioch and magically restoring her lost memory—and then suddenly:

this paragraph of narrative had transported him into a zone beyond his so that he felt as he'd felt now and then as a schoolboy, on the brink of some novelty beyond the temporal, near some life-lifting, -shifting strait of discovery. He had been too clever, crafty, cautious or worldly as a grown man at his work; the minor brilliances, glimpses into the ineffable, had been, properly, lost. (*An After-Dinner's Sleep*, 107)

The writing is austerely careful with those quiet little touches such as 'minor' or 'properly', and the crude enthusiasm is itself subdued; but as George Eliot puts it in *Middlemarch* there is a roar on the other side of its silence. Yet even with this reawakened sense of the extraordinary within the ordinary, as the young and new are felt again within the old and lonely, Alistair knows that these temporary excitements of the mind will in no way alter the course of his life now.

Excited, he jumped to his feet, made to the window with a young man's stride, and there discovered old age again as he rested his forehead on cold glass. (*An After-Dinner's Sleep*, 174)

Reading, even in its uplift or its deepening, cannot be a miracle-cure for the aged or the saddened, nor of course does it bring thoughts that are always guaranteed good or healthy or ethical. But rather, and rightly, it must go on within the ordinary course and linear syntax of a life, including the darkly threatening and dangerous. Yet even the felt return of old age to the reader here is not simple, though indeed inevitable: whatever their content, the varying discoveries and realizations, the turns and returns, comings and the goings in the minds of writers and readers belong to different dimensions from those of merely conventional time or simple story.

3. Conclusions

(i) *The second language*

First, then: concerning that informal and personal under-language, which the reader almost secretly receives from the instigating language on the page.

There is often in its personal message something of the school-kid, the youth, or even the child—but really those are metaphors for anything that lies beneath the assumed stolidity of socially conventional adulthood. This almost primal rawness is to be considered further in the next chapter. But it is worth ending this one with a founding sense of what it is that goes into the development of a reader's use of the space and place that literature allows.

Here is a report on an experiment conducted by child psychologists some years ago. A girl called C, aged 3 years and 7 months, is told a story about a purple elephant who is teased and then shunned by all the other animals because of its strange appearance.[37] 'C' was not yet a reader, and the researcher used toy animals to make the story real to her, inviting 'C' to complete the tale.

'C' at once lay down on the floor, looked the purple elephant in the eye and said, 'I will be your friend, don't be sad.' She then picks it up, taking it out of the situation, and hugs it, adding, 'Now you have a friend'—as if the toy were real, and she knows its feelings, and nothing can hold her back from trying to help it.

This is a very good primal reader at the level of involvement. For 'C' the sheer force of the instinctive emotional identification and intervention make the boundary between story and world, character and herself, humanly non-existent.

But the researcher came back in nineteen months and repeated the experiment when 'C', aged 5 years and 2 months, was now at school, beginning to read and also becoming more socialized. This time 'C' marches the purple elephant over to confront the other animals and tells them they look silly too, 'the tiger with his stripes, the hippopotamus because he's so fat, the giraffe with his long neck':

She has them taunt each other back and forth until the tiger announces that the elephant is right and that it is mean of them to tease him. The tiger says that he is going to be the elephant's friend. Each of the animals moves forward, saying, 'Me too', and the story ends with the elephant giving each of them a ride on its back. (Appleyard, 52)

Manifestly 'C', now at school, is more practised in dealing with the to-and-fro conflicts of a social world. But she is also now more like a writer than a reader: closing off the specialist story-bounds, she can step back less immediately and more indirectly to become a narrator and deviser rather than a participant, turning her sympathy *towards* the elephant into a power *within* it. Yet though she can do far more now both for and with the creature's helplessness, what she does still comes out of that warmed sad flood of feeling she felt at 3.

What goes into being 'a writer' or 'a reader' are therefore inter-related powers and processes long before they become distinct functions or types. Writers depend upon that privately raw-hearted reader we saw developing in the psychologists' experiment, not only as imagined in the outside world but also as lodged still in themselves. That less dignified, more vulnerable person called the-reader-in-themselves—the recipient, that is to say, of the full inner meaning of their own words—is a model of what readers can be at the maximum of response, picking up a tacit second language for themselves on the other side of the formal text.

The example of Dickens in the psychology of grammar

It works like this. The trauma Dickens felt in being sent out to work in a blacking warehouse at the age of 12 is well known now, though he hid it in a private autobiographical fragment during his lifetime:

For many years, when I came near to Robert Warrens' in the Strand, I crossed over to the opposite side of the way, to avoid a certain smell of the cement they put upon the blacking-corks, which reminded me of what I was once. My old way home by the Borough made me cry, after my eldest child could speak.[38]

It is worth noting, in passing, that it is the syntax hingeing on 'after' that is important here: as if to say, 'Though my son comes after me and I of course existed as both child and adult long before he came into being, still I cry like a baby whilst my own baby has long since learnt to talk.' Dickens can barely understand how the two—the child he was and the adult he is—can exist in the same sentence, alongside his unknowing family. Earlier, his own mother and father had not seemed to care that he was sent out to work:

My whole nature was so penetrated with the grief and humiliation of such considerations, that, even now, famous and caressed and happy as I am, I often forget in my dreams that I have a dear wife and children; even that I am a man; and wander desolately back to that time of my life. (Forster, 23)

Now, when Dickens turned this fragment and its memories into the novel *David Copperfield*, an equivalent passage went like this, at the opening of chapter 11:

I know enough of the world now, to have almost lost the capacity of being much surprised by anything; but it is matter of some surprise to me that I can have been so easily thrown away at such an age.

Or more accurately—since I have been educating myself in both composition and reading by examining some of the manuscripts of the great novelists of the nineteenth and twentieth centuries—this is the first version from the manuscript in the Forster Collection of the Victoria and Albert Museum. What Dickens next does, still in the manuscript, is pick up whatever it was that made him write 'almost' ('almost lost the capacity of being much surprised by anything') and insert through its small opening of possibility this little phrase a word or two further on:

but it is matter of some surprise to me, even now, that I can have been so easily thrown away at such an age.

It is the same signature-note '*even now*' that first appeared instinctively in the autobiographical fragment: 'so that even now, famous and caressed and happy as I am, I often forget in my dreams that

I have a dear wife and children...' It was the mark of Dickens's wincing vulnerability to his own words and his own memories, even in imaginative transmutation, and there are many more such inserted on second thought throughout the manuscript—'perhaps' or 'almost' or 'might have been'. Other tiny revisions are like inserting a word like 'something' in place of more definite nouns or more painful explicitness: for example, the word 'it' in describing his ordeal in the factory, 'Whether it lasted for a year, or more, or less, I do not know. I only know *that it was*, and ceased to be' (chapter 14); or the shorthand he uses when he seems to have lost all possibility of love: 'Whatever I might have been to her, [and—*deleted*] or she to me, if I had been more worthy of her long ago, *I was not now, and she was not*' (chapter 58). These delicately implicit little phrases signalled for Dickens himself the triggering of a second language of private and silent memories also characteristic of a sensitive and personally emotional reader. In the psychology of grammar, the work succeeds precisely through the disproportion between the size of the phrase in the sentence—'even now'—and the imagined realization of its meaning and impact elsewhere. Underneath it all and through such little words, the text said tacitly both to Dickens and to the older David, and, almost impossibly, to the little boy they had both been: 'I will be your friend'. There was no one to be friend or father at the time: 'It seems wonderful to me that nobody should have made any sign in my behalf. But none was made' (chapter 11). This is what, without ever looking at the manuscript, Graham Greene had sensed as Dickens's *secret prose*, 'a mind speaking to itself with no one there to listen'.[39] 'No one,' confessed Dickens in his Preface to the 1850 edition of the novel, 'can ever believe this Narrative, in the reading, more than I have believed it in the writing.' Yet the reader (a different form of 'no one', anonymous indeed to Dickens but not uncaring) imaginatively feels this admission as true to what is most deep in the novel.

And the example of Conrad

It is similar with Joseph Conrad in 'Typhoon'. For there in the eye of a storm, the voice of Captain MacWhirr says to his young first mate Jukes, in the raging dark:

'Keep her facing it. They may say what they like, but the heaviest seas run with the wind. Facing it—always facing it—that's the way to get through. You are a young sailor. Face it. That's enough for any man....' ('Typhoon', chapter 5)

Jukes is like the young captain in 'The Shadow Line' on his first voyage in command, fearing instead that he is positively 'shirking it': 'Now I understand that strange sense of insecurity in my past. I always suspected that I might be no good. And here is proof positive. I am shirking it. I am no good.' But so felt Conrad himself at some level. Around the very time he was writing 'Typhoon', Conrad also wrote this in a letter to Edward Garnett, Good Friday, 1899:

The more I write the less substance do I see in my work. The scales are falling off my eyes. It is tolerably awful. And I face it, I face it but the fright is growing on me.[40]

Put the two together, the novella and the letter, and it is as though Conrad was hearing the second in the place of a reader whilst urging the first from the position of writer. The inner cry is: Shirking it. Then: Keep facing it. 'That's enough for *any* man,' wrote Conrad, including himself. And any reader may hear equivalent messages of his or her own from a text. But to Conrad it was strange that what MacWhirr was doing inside his fiction seemed in some sense, maddeningly, more certain and substantial than the writing of the fiction itself. For the strain of writing, said Conrad in *A Personal Record*, a 'material parallel' could only be found in the struggling westward winter passage round Cape Horn: 'but a certain longitude, once won, cannot be disputed,' he wrote, 'whereas a handful of pages, no matter how much you have made them your own, are at best but an obscure and questionable spoil.'[41] This was made worse, more maddeningly circular, if what you were ostensibly writing about *was* the rounding of the Cape, or the going through a storm.

There is a secret human realm that literature serves, and which exists just beneath its texts, where both writers and readers know more of the inner realities of existence than ordinary society lets show.

(ii) *The aesthetic*

My second conclusion on the final meaning of literature as a holding-ground comes out of this, Shakespeare's sonnet 29:

When, in disgrace with fortune and men's eyes,
I all alone beweep my outcast state
And trouble deaf heaven with my bootless cries
And look upon myself and curse my fate,
Wishing me like to one more rich in hope,
Featured like him, like him with friends possess'd,
Desiring this man's art and that man's scope,
With what I most enjoy contented least;
Yet in these thoughts myself almost despising,
Haply I think on thee, and then my state,
Like to the lark at break of day arising
From sullen earth, sings hymns at heaven's gate;
For thy sweet love remember'd such wealth brings
That then I scorn to change my state with kings.

My colleagues and I have offered this poem many times within a range of reading-groups, inside and outside the university. I once even heard the writer Erwin James say that it was this poem that he had sent from his prison to his estranged daughter, with a message to her in the bottle of those last six lines. But whatever the context, it is to the poem's second-half moment of lift-off that readers most often point, as the poem's great change from the depression and self-despair that precedes it.

To get up from the 'sullen earth' of the first movement Shakespeare must work powerfully, characteristically offering a double syntactic value in order to do so: for, fluidly, it is both 'My state ... From sullen earth sings hymns at heaven's gate' and 'Like to the lark at break of day arising | From sullen earth'—the two together for the uplift of the rocket-boost. But what is important, of course, in making the difference is the subliminal effect. One reader on one occasion kept saying beforehand, 'I don't like Shakespeare, I hate Shakespeare from school.' But then of 'Haply I think of thee ...', she said, despite herself, 'I don't like Shakespeare, but that's beautiful', and then again in a different voice within the midst of the reading, more quietly and repeatedly, 'Isn't that lovely, isn't that lovely.'

This is not mere reported sentiment. Research into transcripts from reading-groups indicates (through changes of tone, vocabulary, and body-language, through raised levels of attention and involvement) that whenever anyone finds something 'beautiful', something good is happening that lifts readers and gives them another, cleaner place to be. This surprised our sometimes earnestly puritanical research-group who would normally resist the word 'beautiful', not wanting to be labelled aesthetes, as though we were merely sniffy connoisseurs of 'the flowers of English poesy'. But this is something else because, again on different occasions in different groups, that word 'beautiful' is very quickly associated with the word that frequently follows it: 'lovely'. Some of these group-members are undergoing counselling, suffering from depression or chronic pain. But what a sense of the love-ly offers them is an alternative to the language of therapeutic problem-solving: a beneficent but still neutral, peaceable area that seems to require nothing of them, and has no step-by-step pro-gramme as a result. It already *makes* a change, felt at a specific textual moment to which one can point and return, without demanding a change.

That is why this temporary, contemplative, and experimental holding-ground that literature offers may indeed be usefully identi-fied as 'aesthetic' if we revise the situation of its meaning. In Kierke-gaard's *Fear and Trembling*, the philosopher's great reading of Genesis chapter 22, three major realms of being are identified of which the aesthetic is the lowest. Above the aesthetic is the ethical, and then above all the religious, with Abraham moving beyond the second and into the third, once he begins to obey God's horrific command-ment that he should sacrifice Isaac, his only son. In the midst of this ancient test upon his obedience Abraham still has secret faith that God will not finally require Isaac of him, whilst remaining willing even so to offer his son if that was what was demanded: it is like a simultaneously double sense of things so paradoxical, says Kierke-gaard, that not only can it not be spoken, it can hardly be thought. This point of crisis for Abraham, says Kierkegaard, cannot be medi-ated: Abraham cannot explain or be explained. But this is the tran-scendent moment when, Kierkegaard says, through a particular calling the *individual* must risk setting himself apart from the univer-sal—the norms of human feeling and logic and communication, the collectively assumed category of what is finite reality, and the ethical law itself.

It is a situation to which a modern reader may feel deeply unsympathetic. Kierkegaard himself admits he has never understood how Abraham could go to the very brink of sacrificing the beloved son whose birth he had so long awaited. But this not-understanding, he adds, was emphatically not like the evident difficulties he might have with a complex abstract philosophy such as Hegel's: with Genesis these were to do with a person and his action. This is what makes Kierkegaard a literary thinker, like a novelist outside the novel. In Hegel the inexplicable looked inexplicable but in Abraham the inexplicable was not in any language, but in the simple fact of Abraham's silently embodied faith in going through with the offering to the point when at the very last moment God stayed his hand. However terrible the scene, this is in Kierkegaard human thinking, thought questioningly embedded in the human, in character and story and scenario, with all the difficulty of thinking himself *into* Abraham. And Kierkegaard does not take the easy way out through simply distancing the great things within the realm of cultural history and contextualized explanation. 'I prefer to talk of what Abraham did,' he says, 'not as though it were thousands of years ago but in the light of my reading it now, as if it happened yesterday, letting only the greatness itself be the distance.' This, characteristically, is the realm and stance of a bold personal reader.

But with his emphasis on the religious transcendence of the ethical, of the individual transcendence of the universal, albeit in fear and trembling, Kierkegaard finally and decisively relegates the role of the aesthetic to a lowly place. In the aesthetic stage of existence, he says, the play of possibility is placed above the ties of actuality. Ever fleeing from what is boring, restlessly seeking what is interesting regardless of ethics, the ego of the aesthetic type immerses itself in the present immediacy of the sensuous and sensual world.

But what I have been arguing in this chapter is that if literature is indeed the realm of the aesthetic, then the aesthetic so far from being the lowest of the three stages is more like an agnostic holding-ground between the ethical and the religious, retaining nonetheless the sense of presentness which Kierkegaard attributes to it even in its lower manifestations. I don't think literature can be moralistic, says one; says another, religious thinking no longer has a place in modern literature. But as with the zones in Doris Lessing's *Marriages*, those other realms do not remain secure and separate outside the aesthetic: along with other disciplines and alternative frameworks, they seek their origins, their place, their justification again within it. For searchers, the aesthetic is the present site of experience and of experiment and of meaning, prior to the re-evolution of verbal definitions or firm categories.

(iii) Not system but ethos

There is one further corollary. This chapter has been about those resonant places where in the words of Johnson a reader can sense 'systems in their elements', 'actions in their motives', and see how far they can be given a language and a syntax through which to be further spelt out. But what emphatically is not on offer here is a systematic scheme or programme for reading.

Literary thinking, thinking in and through literature, is not a system but it is an ethos, an invisible place of disposition that nonetheless exists. For an ethos is to a form of endeavour what a resonance is in surrounding the words of a text: it signals something more than the merely literal. Without ever being able or willing to spell itself out fully, an ethos extends the moment of resonance or realization into a tacit way of being—a way of thinking and feeling, of imagining and doing, in the world.

An idea at its deepest has more than just a statable content. There is a tone or temper of mind in which a particular idea or belief is held. The thought of it is nuanced: it has its own vibratory feel and its own implicit pulsation, blending and mingling with the mood and character of the person who holds it. Hold it in the wrong way and the spirit of its meaning may be distorted and destroyed. Hold it in the right way and the thought and its thinker are united and fulfilled in each other. That is why it is significant when a voice changes in the very process of reading aloud. For some thoughts create the right ethos in those who can tune into them.

I shall have more to say of this ethos of meaning in Chapters 2 and 3.

Notes

1. Marcel Proust, 'Poetry, or the Mysterious Laws', in *Against Sainte-Beuve and Other Essays*, trans. John Sturrock (London: Penguin, 1988), 149.
2. See chapter 5 of J. S. Mill's *Autobiography* (1873) and also George Mac-Donald's essay 'Wordsworth's Poetry' in his *Dish of Orts* (1893).
3. Henri Bergson, *Creative Evolution*, trans. Arthur Mitchell (London: Macmillan, 1914), 49.
4. Marilynne Robinson, *The Death of Adam* (New York: Picador, 1998), 78.
5. See Keith Oatley, *Such Stuff as Dreams* (Oxford: Wiley-Blackwell, 2011), 206–7 on the work of Lisa Aziz-Zadeh; also GuillaumeThierry, Clara D. Martin, Victorina Gonzalez-Diaz, Roozbeh Rezaie, Neil Roberts, and Philip Davis, 'Event-Related Potential Characterisation of the Shakespearean Functional Shift in Narrative Sentence Structure', *NeuroImage* 40 (2008), 923–31.
6. Quoted in Maryanne Wolf's admirable book *Proust and the Squid* (Cambridge: Icon, 2008), 143.
7. William James, *The Principles of Psychology*, first published 1890, 2 vols. (New York: Dover Publications, 1950), i. 251. Hereafter cited as 'PP'.
8. From his *Problems of Life and Mind*, quoted in Rick Rylance, *Victorian Psychology and British Culture 1850–1880* (Oxford: Oxford University Press, 2000), 136.
9. This profoundly encouraging formulation is Michael Polanyi's in *Knowing and Being* (London: Routledge & Kegan Paul, 1969), 131.
10. The first surviving version, held by the Wordsworth Trust, goes thus, more explicitly:

> Long time before her head lay low
> Dead to the world was she:
> But now she's in her grave, and Oh!
> The difference to me!

11. I am indebted here to Simon Jarvis, *Wordsworth's Philosophic Song* (Cambridge: Cambridge University Press, 2006), 25–8.
12. *The Prose Works of William Wordsworth*, ed. W. J. B. Owen and Jane Worthington Smyser, 3 vols. (Oxford: Clarendon Press, 1974), ii. 93.
13. See *The Varieties of Religious Experience* (1903), lecture 10.
14. R. G. Collingwood, *The Principles of Art*, first published 1938 (Oxford: Oxford University Press, 1958), 109. I am indebted here to Oatley, *Such Stuff as Dreams*, 129–30.
15. *Elizabethan Critical Essays*, ed. G. Gregory Smith, 2 vols. (Oxford: Oxford University Press), i. 185.
16. *A Defence of Rhyme* (1610) in *Elizabethan Critical Essays*, ii. 366.
17. *Coleridge on Shakespeare*, ed.Terence Hawkes (Harmondsworth: Penguin, 1969), 229.

18. John Ruskin, *Modern Painters*, vol. ii (1846), part 3, section 2, chapter 3, paras. 4–5.

19. Michael Wood, *Literature and the Taste of Knowledge* (Cambridge: Cambridge University Press, 2005), 41.

20. See for example Ken Robinson, *The Element* (London: Penguin, 2009): 'When we are in our Element, we feel we are doing what we are meant to be doing and being who we're meant to be...There's a real sense of ideas flowing through you and out of you; that you're in some way channeling these things. You're being an instrument of them rather than being obstructive to them or struggling to reach them.... [People] are literally more alive because of it' (90–1, 93).

21. D. H. Lawrence, *Phoenix* (London: Heinemann, 1936), 431.

22. Russell Hoban, *Fremder* (London: Jonathan Cape, 1996), 78.

23. See Philip Davis, 'Syntax and Pathways', *Interdisciplinary Science Reviews* 33.4 (2008), 265–77.

24. Joseph Gold in his unjustly neglected work *The Story Species* (Ontario: Fitzhenry & Whiteside, 2002), xv, 19, 41.

25. Hannah Arendt, *The Life of the Mind* (San Diego: Harcourt, 1978), i. 179–93.

26. Quoted in John Henry Newman, *An Essay on the Development of Christian Doctrine*, 1878 edition, ed. Ian Ker (Notre Dame, Ind.: University of Notre Dame Press, 1989), xxiv. Hereafter cited as *Development*.

27. See Iain McGilchrist, *The Master and his Emissary* (New Haven: Yale University Press, 2009).

28. John Henry Newman, *University Sermons*, 1826–43 (London: SPCK, 1970), 325 (sermon 15). Hereafter cited as *University Sermons*.

29. John Coulson, *Religion and Imagination* (Oxford: Clarendon Press, 1981), epigraph.

30. All quotations taken from *The Rambler*, ed. W. J. Bate and A. B. Strauss, vols. iii–v in *The Yale Edition of the Works of Samuel Johnson* (New Haven: Yale University Press, 1969).

31. Quoted in Frank Doherty, *Samuel Beckett* (London: Hutchinson, 1971), 88. Thus Beckett: 'It's Johnson, always Johnson, who is with me. And if I follow any tradition it is his' (120).

32. Saul Bellow, *Herzog*, first published 1964 (Harmondsworth: Penguin, 1965), 189.

33. Quoted in *Johnson on Johnson*, ed. John Wain (London: Dent, 1976), ix–x.

34. Edmund Burke, *Reflections on the Revolution in France* (1790), ed. C. C. O'Brien (Harmondsworth: Penguin, 1968), 152–3. See my 'Johnson's Cosmology: Vacuity and Ramification', in Liam Gearon (ed.), *English Literature, Theology and the Curriculum* (London: Cassell, 1999), 173–89.

35. Stanley Middleton, *An After-Dinner's Sleep* (London: Hutchinson, 1986), 18–19; hereafter cited as *An After-Dinner's Sleep*.

36. *The Life and Work of Thomas Hardy*, first published 1928, 1930 as written by Florence Emily Hardy, ed. Michel Millgate (London: Macmillan, 1984), 151.

37. W. George Scarlett and Dennie Wolf, 'When It's Only Make-Believe: The Construction of a Boundary between Fantasy and Reality in Story-telling' (1979), in J. A. Appleyard, *Becoming A Reader* (Cambridge: Cambridge University Press, 1994), 51–3; hereafter cited as Appleyard.

38. John Forster, *The Life of Charles Dickens*, first published 3 vols. 1872–4, ed. A. J. Hoppé, 2 vols. (London: Everyman's Library, Dent, 1966), i. 33; hereafter cited as Forster.

39. Graham Greene, *The Lost Childhood and Other Essays* (London: Eyre and Spottiswoode, 1951), 53.

40. Quoted in Frederick R. Karl, *Joseph Conrad: The Three Lives* (London: Faber, 1979), 485.

41. Joseph Conrad, *A Personal Record*, first published 1912, in *A Personal Record & The Mirror of the Sea*, ed. M. Kalnins (London: Penguin, 1998), 95.

2
An Awakened Sense of Being

Introduction

Why might people need the holding-ground that literature offers? This chapter examines the extra potential dimensions, the exploratory in-between areas, and (in short) the quickened and deepened inner life for readers within the ethos of that holding-ground.

The sense of primary realities

William James said that the challenge that Tolstoy provided lay in his being 'one of those primitive oaks of men', a man with 'the aboriginal human marrow' in his bones, who could not be satisfied with the second-order insincerities and falsehoods of so-called polite civilization.[1]

Tolstoy created in his character Levin a version of this original type, albeit a man less intimidating than his creator. For Levin is one who is awake to the reality of *first* things, like the vulnerable sneeze of his new-born baby, and of *last* things, the voice of the dying brother who, pronounced dead, still whispers, 'Not yet'. But in between the two, in the middle of things, he is also a person who feels all at sea—like a man, says Tolstoy, who having admired beforehand, on-shore, the secure and easy motion of a boat on the water, had actually got into that boat and found it quite different. That is indeed the territory of the nineteenth-century realist novel in which, for example, Levin himself cannot understand someone like his old friend Sviyazhsky, a man who thinks like a radical liberal but operates in his work and in his family like a dull conservative. 'What is the connection between that man's life and his thoughts?' Levin asks himself, like an innocent. For Levin is Tolstoy's doggedly idealistic Everyman, who down to the very roots of the personal is representative of a sense of the absolute and the primal however obscured, entangled, or misplaced in the confusions of the human world. In his mind Levin asks both of Sviyazhsky and of himself, those obstinate questionings that, on a very different occasion, the young Wordsworth in 'Resolution and Independence' kept asking of a common peasant-figure, who seemed to have some fundamental good in him which the poet himself had not: 'How is it that you live, and what is it you do?'

Tolstoy's novella *Death of Ivan Ilyich* precisely enacts the radical shift from an existence formed by a secondary set of social expectations and conventions to the naked plight of the solitary individual who, faced with his own mortality, is forced to ask himself fundamental questions. 'What is it you want?' asks some inner voice Ivan Ilyich has never heard before his illness 'To live? Live how?' As Ivan tries to say to himself in defence and denial, he has been after all a successful professional lawyer, has lived to a prosperous middle age, has married well enough and raised a suitable family, much like Levin's Sviyazhsky. By such mental screens, says Tolstoy, the sick man tries in vain to keep away the thought of death, and with it the thought of a life wasted; but 'the same thought—it wasn't just a thought but something that seemed like reality—kept coming back and facing him'.

For those who feel institutionalized or conventionalized, existence is like living in the dark shelter of Plato's cave shut out from the original light of reality. This chapter is about a primary feeling of ontological reality awakened in literature and through literature, in place of the sense of a second-rate, low-affect world of the merely routine or automatic. That is to say: the coming to life of things— places, people, ideas, feelings, objects, issues—as substantively felt and compelling realities tested out in the reading present. There, realities *exceed* the extent to which they are named or known. Ontology *before* epistemology is the law of life here. 'It wasn't just a thought but something that seemed like reality.'

In what follows, in the making of this claim for an awakened ontology,[2] my opening section, 'How First Things Last', is essentially about the uses of trouble or crisis in disclosing the sense of a primary reality; whereas section two, 'The Middle of Things', is more concerned with the sudden presence of surprise and change and shift.

But in the chapter as a whole it is the complex interrelation of first and last and midst that marks out the contemplative work to be done within literature's holding-ground. This chapter attempts to rescue reading from institutionalization by maintaining the instincts of emotional recognition within what is nonetheless the discipline of attentive deciphering.

1. How first things last

The cry

A fine poem by Les Murray entitled 'An Absolutely Ordinary Rainbow' tells the story of a man found inexplicably crying aloud in the midst of a busy main-street in Sydney. The word goes round: 'There's a fellow weeping down there. No one can stop him.' A crowd of amazed onlookers gathers around him:

> The man we surround, the man no one approaches
> simply weeps, and does not cover it, weeps
> not like a child, not like the wind, but like a man
> and does not declaim it, nor beat his breast, nor even
> sob very loudly—yet the dignity of his weeping
>
> holds us back from his space, the hollow he makes about him
> in the midday light, in his pentagram of sorrow...

That between-stanza space ('the dignity of his weeping | holds us back') has to do with all I have tried to say in Chapter 1 about creating attentive places for the resonance of what matters. Within such a place this man of Murray's could be a prophet, in a lamentation like Jeremiah's:

Is it nothing to you, all ye that pass by? behold, and see if there be any sorrow like unto my sorrow, which is done unto me...

—could even be in imitation of Christ, when the shortest verse in the whole Bible says, simply and barely, 'Jesus wept'—'an *argument*', said John Donne in a sermon preached in Whitehall, Lent 1622, 'of his being man'. Or equally of course this is a place that also admits the thought that he could just be a person in the midst of nervous breakdown, a lunatic even. But perhaps most of all, that unnamed man in the street is also the poet, standing for what being a poet has to mean in his emotional representativeness, with the on-looking crowd as his readers.

Les Murray knows well enough how poetry, like crying, can be dismissed as a soft or childish or gendered thing, as though best left to the women to feel for rather than the conventionally tough (non-reading) male. But this unmanned man here, outside those grotesque stereotypes and all the more human for it, has in his weeping a primal language of sheer physically feeling presence, an 'argument' for being that is existent before any words and upsets all kinds:

> and many weep for sheer acceptance, and more
> refuse to weep for fear of all acceptance,
> but the weeping man, like the earth, requires nothing,
> the man who weeps ignores us, and cries out
> of his writhen face and ordinary body
>
> not words but grief, not messages but sorrow
> hard as the earth, sheer, present as the sea—

In memory of this primal elemental language, Murray's words of poetry are made into a discrete and protected place for their version of weeping out loud: the poem differs from the life it here describes only in being without the threat of utter public exposure, as well as without the severance of private concealment.

In that urban space in Sydney the people don't know what to do, how or if to help; but their attention remains held nonetheless. In a world of hidden and denied emotions only some of the bystanders feel able to receive from the man what the poem calls 'the gift of weeping'. Others in the crowd, still looking on at the silent man who seeks no help, find their minds 'longing for tears as children for a rainbow', sun within rain, the good inside the painful.

'There is a crust about the impressible parts of men's minds,' wrote John Ruskin in *The Seven Lamps of Architecture*, 'which must be pierced through before they can be touched to the quick; and though we may prick at it in a thousand separate places, we might as well have let it alone if we do not come through somewhere with a deep thrust' ('The Lamp of Power').

Poetry is the great articulate cry. 'Dispute it like a man,' urges Shakespeare's Malcolm: 'But I must also feel it as a man,' replies Macduff. Sometimes in the strain of his life it was as though Ruskin himself might have stood bare-headed in the city streets, in all the reactive danger of the evangelical spirit in which he was raised, crying like Lear:

> Howl, howl, howl! O you are men of stones,
> Had I your tongues and eyes, I'd use them so
> That heaven's vaults should crack.
>
> *(King Lear* 5.3 231–3)

At the very least for Ruskin, if the heavens will not crack, the human carapace should. Literature, he believed, must reverse human hardening, reminding the people of their first hearts, lost in secondary concealments and protections.

But when, more quietly and requiring nothing, Murray's man weeps in public, there are also two things he does *not* do which he might have. He does not cry like a child, though the crowd in response long for tears as a child for a rainbow. Nor does he call to a God, but when he stops weeping hurries away 'evading believers'. Yet these two different primary things that he does *not* do border close upon what he does. Implicitly they help define poetry by the primal human impulses of crying and calling which it both draws upon and transfigures. Some poems, like this one in my experience, seem to hold founding thoughts and deep cultural memories like genes, so to speak, within the very biology of their individual makeup. I want to register such resonances not in abstraction but through Donne's version of what 'argument' is: specific embodied instances of fundamental impulses which this poem seems to recall.

The child in us

First, the presence of the (lost) child.

George Eliot's young Maggie Tulliver in *The Mill on the Floss* (1860) often finds her emotions *bursting* out of her like tears themselves, as if she were not yet strong enough to contain them within herself, and the strength of her lay rather in the emotional forces themselves; as though she intuitively believed, moreover, that her emotions belonged not just within her own self but out in the world that seemed to cause them. For the child the pain and the despair are absolute:

Very trivial, perhaps, this anguish seems to weather-worn mortals who have to think of Christmas bills, dead loves and broken friendships, but it was not less bitter to Maggie—perhaps it was even more bitter—than what we are fond of calling the real troubles of mature life. 'Ah, my child, you will have real troubles to fret about by and by,' is the consolation we have almost all of us had administered to us in our childhood, and have repeated to other children since we have been grown up. (volume i, chapter 7)

You lose sight of your mother in some strange new place; schoolfellows shut you out of their game; a brother or sister or best friend scorns you. Though adults may tell you that you will get over such things, these momentary experiences of snub or parting can seem like total and unique losses, with no equipment in us yet to make them customary or passing. Such absolute moments, says George Eliot, leave their trace and live in us still, 'but such traces have blent themselves irrecoverably with the firmer texture of our youth and manhood; and so it comes that we can look on at the troubles of our children with a smiling unbelief in the reality of their pain.' That is the adult way: that absolutes turn out to become relative in the blend. 'This too shall pass' says the ancient Sufi proverb. Whatever it is, the crowd in the Sydney street will have tried of course to get over it—the sane survival mechanism of living on in time, however half-knowingly damaged. Which also means getting over that childhood state to which trouble sometimes seems to reduce us. 'Move on' and 'Get closure' are the great buzz phrases of the self-help manuals. But the idea of getting over it, even in the very midst of the experience, is itself part of the equivocal pain of semi-denial, to make the thing mean and matter less.

But my point is not just about childhood grief; it is about childhood utterance and expression.

Charles Fernyhough is both an academic psychologist and a novelist who combined the two in a memoir of the development of his own daughter, from birth to aged 3. In *The Baby in the Mirror* (2008) one of his central interests is what he calls 'private speech' when little children speak their thoughts out loud, when they play, with their thoughts audibly spilling out into the world in a busy unselfconsciousness that comes from there being no finished self yet in place.

His 17-month daughter, for example, is trying to fit brightly coloured animal pieces—dog, duck, teddy bear, bee—into the corresponding shapes in a wooden board, her mother in attendance as a helping adjunct to her efforts. As she turns over a piece from the pile, the child names it and, encouraged by the mother, says what sound it makes. But there is a moment when she can't get the fish to fit in. 'In' she says as if entreating it; then in her effort, 'Hard.' Ferny-hough believes this last is a genuine borderline-moment: partly a request for external help, he says ('Can't you see how hard this is?'), but also at the same time an internal note for herself. Her mother helps her but she also struggles with the next piece: 'Um, bit hard' she says as she tries changing her posture to get the piece in. 'It's very hard, that one,' her mother agrees. This is, says Fernyhough, not just parental sympathy but an aspect of shared thinking, thinking that is actually happening out there in the world *between* people in the shaping and maturing of intelligence. Soon the parent will only hear the child talk her thoughts aloud, includ-ing her own versions of the parental voice ('Come on, you'll be alright'), when the parent is still in earshot but no longer immedi-ately by. What is caught in action here is the process of developing internalization.

Thus the larger point I want to emphasize, still in relation to Les Murray's poem, concerns the gradual human movement from out-side in: the transitional movement from a blurted so-called 'private' speech, where thought is still spoken out loud, to 'inner' speech, in which thought becomes silent and separated within an internal iden-tity. When that movement is complete, when the boundaries be-tween within and without are beginning to get established, there is, as so often, at once gain and loss. For a little time, the parents will still hear their child directly thinking aloud, spilling the thoughts into the world. Thereafter, though the created inner life and identity are emphatically an achievement not to be denied or regretted, sharing becomes quite different.

What the parents first heard was (as A. S. Byatt so beautifully describes it in her novel *Still Life*) a new voice pronouncing the old words, where before there had been no voice but only a wail or snuffle. Never such innocence again, as another poet says. For later, as the child's thoughts become inner and separate, it is the lost shared outerness that the parents must register, even whilst half-trying to resist their nostalgia. At an equivalent moment of development, C. Day-Lewis writes this to his son, and perhaps even more to his own now lonely memory, in 'Walking Away':

> I can see
> You walking away from me towards the school
> With the pathos of a half-fledged thing set free
> Into a wilderness, the gait of one
> Who finds no path where the path should be.

'I have had worse partings,' says the poet. But 'that hesitant figure', he writes, 'Has something I never quite grasp to convey | About nature's give-and-take':

> How selfhood begins with a walking away,
> And love is proved in the letting go.

Poetry is often about such informal changes, helpless ruptures, and inevitable, acceptable losses—formless until poetry gives them the *form* that life-in-passing seems hardly to acknowledge.

What is more, such poetry re-creates in its own way something of the lost realm of private outer thought lodged in between the social and the internal. It is not, of course, exactly the child's uncensored and spilt formative thinking, a magical openness onto the world. But it is an inner voice also simultaneously outside itself, on paper. Silently reading, you hear its voice inside your own head as if aloud yet transplanted. However, its utterance must also now bear the demands of adulthood. These include what Wordsworth in his 'Immortality Ode' called 'thoughts that do often lie too deep for tears'; and Day-Lewis's father-figure is, still tearfully, on the verge of that understanding. For this is writing that begins from the depths of silence, when direct speaking fails and crying must stop.

The plea and the prayer—the Psalmist

This brings me to the second great primal element suggested by 'An Absolutely Ordinary Rainbow': the direct cry for (missing) help.

In a strange and flawed little book called *Beyond* which he wrote towards the end of his life, aged 81, I. A. Richards argued for the closeness of the cry of prayer to the sources of poetry. Richards was one of the great founding figures of literary criticism in the 1920s, when the new discipline of closely attentive reading seemed at the very forefront of academic thought, and literature a central subject in a way that perhaps has never quite been maintained or recovered in the universities since. In *Beyond* it is the psalms to which Richards turns for their having become, ever since their translation into the vernacular, the collective cultural model for the lonely cry of Everyman. But what within them Richards concentrates upon is what technically in rhetoric is known as 'apostrophe'—the sudden turning away from the ordinary course of a speech to address some person or object, present or (more usually) absent. Here, for example, is Psalm 42 (3–7):

> My tears have been my meat day and night, while they continually say unto me, Where is thy God?
> When I remember these things, I pour out my soul in me...
> Why art thou cast down, O my soul? And why art thou disquieted in me?
> Hope thou in God: for I shall yet praise him for the help of his countenance.
> O my God, my soul is cast down within me

There is a kind of reader who argues that human beings have cried to God because they have not been able to help themselves. Consequently they have had to invent someone or something to cry *to*, in lieu of action, instead of finding nothing. 'Where is now my God?' But the sort of reader I try for in my own teaching is one who also wants to know what the meaning might be like from the *inside* of somebody else's belief or situation. For such a reader, regardless of professed belief or unbelief, it is the subtle little intricately changing prepositions in Psalm 42 that seem implicit signs of some larger framework of understanding than that of the modern self.

For these subtle prepositions deny that this is (as the reductionist might say) no more than a man merely talking '*to himself*'. First, the text of the Psalmist says: My tears—the tears that are in me or burst out of me—call '*unto* me'. That is to say, the emotions bear messages both from me and then back to me at another level. And as I, the Psalmist, listen to their cry, they make me 'pour *out* my soul *in* me'—as though my *soul* (or heart, in the translation in the Book of Common Prayer) were a deeper version of my *tears* now released in response to them. But in the next move it is I who then cry back to

my own soul, asking: Why art thou disquieted *in* me? And finally if
my soul, not answering, will not turn itself to hope in God, I have
to do so in its stead. I have cried *to* my soul as it has cried *in* me,
but now I cry *for* my soul *to* my God: 'O my God, my soul is cast
down within me.' I know these are tiny intricacies of reading, but
'See God in small,' said Lancelot Andrewes, one of the great team
of translators that made the King James Bible, 'or you will never see
Him in large.' It is not just true of a God.

'Deep calleth unto deep' the Psalmist says (42:7), as he stands by
the river of Jordan and its waterfalls. But it is not just that the deep-
in-him calls out to the deep outside or beyond, as if in lost corre-
spondence. A sense of the deep-from-without is also what sets the
deep-in-him crying for it in the first place. The cries are not just of
the soul, they are (as it were) the cries of God not being there, seeking to preserve the relationship even by calling. The Psalmist makes
one further final venture in lament, resolving to turn direct to God
in his own voice:

I will say unto God my rock, Why hast thou forgotten me? why go I in
mourning because of the oppression of the enemy?

Again a sceptical reader may well object in the name of conventional logic: what is the use of crying to Him at the fact that He does
not hear your cries, when this cry is just another of them? But that
is what the word 'thou' is for: 'Why hast thou forgotten me? Why
hast thou forsaken me?' It won't give up by using the word 'he' instead. It still makes of language an act of calling, in the hope of
being heard and of being spoken to.

What deeply interested the aged I. A. Richards was not just the
ancient cry to God, made even in moving defiance of its own apparent unavailingness. It was that the call to God was emblematic of *all*
discourse which, in the face of loss or absence or need, has finally to
attempt the impossible or the contradictory utterance. Otherwise
the heart or soul would be utterly silenced in despair. What Richards thought to be one of the great first acts in creative human utterance was the address to a missing Thou of any kind, in any form.
'I can see | You walking away from me.' This—the call unanswered
but still calling—seems close to the origin of poetry and its implicit
continuing purpose in existence.

Reading the religious...?

In *Mr Sammler's Planet*, Saul Bellow's Sammler, a Holocaust survivor who does not think of himself as a religious man, does not know why he keeps reading and returning to medieval religious texts. It is not that he wants to hitch a ride on the language of a belief he does not actually hold. Nor is his a curatorial concern that if modern people cannot read religious writing any more then much of human literature is lost to them, and will be lost ever increasingly in future. What moves him is rather what made William James write *The Varieties of Religious Experience*: that there is something in this, even if we do not formally believe in it, even though we do not know how to translate it; something of deep primal importance even if finally we have to leave it behind.

It is towards the strange deep old texts that Sammler is drawn. Long tendentious arguments and reductive explanations are what, Sammler says, he finds too much around and about him. The old man is tired of their coercive pigeonholing, their constant thinness, and their passing fashion. He wants instead descriptions of experience to carry in his head, without being told what to make of them. Weary of modern noise, he wants succinct and austere sayings that stay in mind like poetry. 'This too shall pass.' What draws Sammler to these religious works, even as a non-believer, is a dissatisfaction related to Saul Bellow's own sense that modern people may be trapped in a false and over-familiar framework, by an impoverished world-view. As if they might need a different model of self and a deeper psychological vocabulary to accompany an alternative ontology. 'I am,' cried the poet Cowper, 'a stranger to the system I inhabit.'

What Saul Bellow feared was that the cry would not be made any more if it seemed melodramatic, stupid or pointless, and meaning-lessly out-of-date.

The example of Johnson's sinner

It is not difficult to understand how very hard it may be from within the middle of things to extricate a lost voice in a lost cause. Here is an example even from an age still imbued with the possibility of prayer, confession, and repentance. It is the story of one who would not cry in the street, and could hardly pray to God, but felt he had

betrayed all that he had previously meant to be. His name was William Dodd

Samuel Johnson once wrote the most final of all his sermons as a
proxy for Dodd who was a disgraced clergyman sentenced to death
for forgery. It was a sermon of ultimate repentance to be delivered
by Dodd to his fellow-prisoners, in his last office as a cleric. But
nearing the eve of execution Dodd felt too guilty, too fearful, and
too disgraced to write it, as though he were doubly defeated—first
by what he himself had done, and then again by what the shameful
thought of it despairingly disabled him from now doing. We know
a lot in our own time about the disgrace of public figures caught in
scandal and hypocrisy, about repentances or atonements that would
never have been thought of if the culprit had not been found out.
But Johnson knew that repentance had to pray for its very possibility
even against itself. He gave Dodd, like some fallen Adam, the language in which to say that almost impossible thing when the Cretan
liar now claims he is finally speaking the truth.

The shortness of the time which is before us, gives little power, even to
ourselves, of distinguishing the effects of terror from those of conviction; of
deciding, whether our present sorrow for sin proceeds from abhorrence of
guilt, or dread of punishment; whether the violence of our inordinate passions be totally subdued by fear of God, or only crushed and restrained by
the temporary force of present calamity.

He writes '*even to ourselves*'—'we' here are the condemned, who
ought perhaps to be the best judges of our own inner sincerity at
the last, were we not certainly our most biasedly self-interested
witnesses too. The fallen prose of the self-damaged and the self-
disauthenticating had to spell all this out, as poetry might not,
struggling at 'distinguishing' and 'deciding' one thing from another,
in a tarnished analysis of a complex and dubious context. And in
hiddenly writing it Johnson really did mean those words 'us' and
'our' and 'ourselves', for he feared in himself also such natural
hypocrisy. 'I am almost afraid to renew my resolutions', he wrote
in his private prayers and diaries at Easter 1765, thinking of how
often in the past he had made his contrite vows and then broken
them. '*Almost* afraid', and yet he did renew them, just as he asked
Dodd to pray for him too when he handed the sermon over.

In such confessions, offered here as another prime type of literature, humans don't know if they mean what they utter; they would be bound to think they did; and they cannot trust what they are bound to want to think, though equally they cannot trust their despair either. In that self-implicatedness everything must suffer in acting, act in suffering.[3] For here lies the human interest—in the middle earth's refusal either wholly to deny its erring and its helplessness or completely to succumb to them; in that rich deep area created by the continuous interchange between passive and active which marks out the human situation.

And all the time amidst the infinite regressions of thought upon thought, it makes no difference: we, Dodd's audience, are going to die and somewhere, even if we ourselves never find it, there should be the real truth of ourselves and what we are and mean. The task of writing is to put it all forward, saturating the solution, in evidence both for and against till we hardly know the difference. That *is* writing at the confessed maximum of its self-known limitation, leaving itself as a personal thing now, an existence, just short of the final judgement. 'Let me not love thee, if I love thee not,' wrote George Herbert in restless relation to his troublesome God.

> Yet, though thou troublest me, I must be meek;
> In weakness must be stout.
> Well, I will change the service, and go seek,
> Some other master out.
> Ah my dear God! Though I am clean forgot,
> Let me not love thee, if I love thee not.
> (Herbert, 'Affliction I')

It is like Ben Jonson in his grief-ridden poem 'To Heaven', fearing lest it be thought 'these prayers be | For weariness of life, not love of thee.' No one knows how wholly sincere he or she is; everyone knows the ulterior motivations one always has. Even the wish to be sincere may be insufficiently no more than second-order. But what these poets have is the clean sense of an ultimate reality before the imagined eyes of which they work to yield up everything only then to let it stand, in that middle realm of being. The achievement of the human cry is both active and suffering.

Prayer become poetry's cry

But even in a secular world without a prayer, that is where the most serious writing still stands: *in medias res*, in an appeal that, short of certain truth, or final judgement, or a missing God, nonetheless posits or imagines that degree of serious effort at witness. This is why I. A. Richards was interested in poems unconsummated by external answers or responses. The poem could be to a dead spouse or a distant loved one, to a memory of place or happening, in mitigation of loss or in celebration of recall.

In any such case Richards offers a shorthand gnomic formula for what goes on in such work. It was this: that what the lines are speaking *of*, says Richards, becomes immediately and literally that *to* which they are spoken, and that *for* which they speak. It is like (paradoxically) telling your dead father or lost husband or grown-up son that he is not there with you when you most need him. This is the double loss of those to whom you would now turn for help in such bereavement were they not also the ones who had died. You speak of them, you speak to them even of themselves, and you speak for them even to yourself—and all in that arguably irrational but primal intuition which is built into the very use of language: namely, that such speaking, as it goes forth into the air, is also the hope of being spoken *to*, in return.

So for example—my example—a four-line poem by George Crabbe written on the death of his wife, Sarah. The two had met and become engaged when he was 18. She then waited more than ten years for him to establish himself. They were married for thirty years when she died in 1813 after much illness, physical and mental, following the death of one of their sons in 1796. 'His Late Wife's Wedding-Ring':

> The ring, so worn as you behold,
> So thin, so pale, is yet of gold:
> The passion, such it was to prove;
> Worn with life's cares, love yet was love.

This is, first, a poem written *on* or *of* 'the ring', though the ring, now left behind, is of course naturally reminiscent of his dead wife, not least in that (doubly) 'worn' state of being 'thin' and 'pale'—as she herself must have been in the later years.

But second, it is also written *to* the ring, as the widower seems meditatively to turn it round and round in his fingers ('*so* worn ... *so* thin, *so* pale'), the object coming to life 'yet' for being left there as a memory in place of 'her', the lost 'thou' who continually wore it. For poetry is that kind of ontological awakening (not just a knowing it and a describing it) when things become really the most of themselves through the attention of human consciousness and human recognition.

Thirdly, however, the poem is written finally *for* the sake of the ring and what it represents even without its owner. Amidst the bereft silence, and in all its right to a consciously disproportionate brevity, the poem is to speak on behalf of the marriage the ring betokened. The ring marks and keeps the promise that the originating 'passion' of youth should give way to nothing less than 'love' through the years. For like the marriage, the poem keeps its word: '*love* yet was *love*'. But also, in counterpart to that affirmation, though the ring '*is yet* of gold', the final tense must recognize death if not defeat: 'love *yet was* love'. It is like the mother's wedding ring in Tony Harrison's poem 'Timer' which survives her cremation. Such poetry exists in that inextricable middle earth which, I am arguing, is the literary domain, pitched between the dependent and the creative, the helplessness and the effort.

In similar spirit, there are those wonderful lines from Bishop Henry King's 'Exequy' to his own dead wife in the tomb—written to 'thee', when to put 'her' would be to lose her twice over:

> Thou wilt not wake
> Till I thy fate shall overtake:
> Till age, or grief, or sickness must
> Marry my body to that dust
> It so much loves; and fill the room
> My heart keeps empty in thy Tomb.
> Stay for me there; I will not fail
> To meet thee in that hollow Vale.
> And think not much of my delay;
> I am already on the way

Ageing and dying are of course helplessly passive; but here love makes them as though they were now also willing things in him, loving and active, in the journey to joining and re-marrying her. It is beautiful that through the simple intimate tones of their shared earthly life—stay for me, wait for me, I will not fail—he not only imagines her but imagines her thinking of him. That is the great poetic loop: the beyond held within; the within pulled beyond.

'Instead of flowers [he writes to her], accept these words:

> Receive a strew of weeping verse
> From thy griev'd friend, whom thou might'st see
> Quite melted into tears for thee.
> Dear loss! Since thy untimely fate
> My task hath been to meditate
> On thee, on thee: thou art the book,
> The library whereon I look
> Though almost blind.'

He is that friend, that reader of her past life. And thinking of himself as 'thy friend' is far better than his simply writing 'me'. In literature there is something important about writers taking back *in* what they have just given out, as they go along from phrase to phrase and line to line: 'on thee, on thee'. That is to say, 'thy griev'd friend' offers a steadying distance from 'me' but a distance across which almost immediately he receives back from 'her' the imagination of her seeing him. 'Whom thou might'st see | Quite melted into tears': *might* (because that is what I am often like now) *if* you were still with me. And those tender places where the verse turns in that way into a half line—'From thy griev'd friend', 'Though almost blind', 'It so much loves', 'Stay for me there'—are like a restrained representation of loving tears not to be exposed in public. It is part of what in the previous chapter I described as a secret second language-within-language, that such half-lines should regularly come at the beginning of a line that seems only to come afterwards, stopped short but left-over: 'that dust/It so much loves'.

> Dear (forgive
> The crime) I am content to live
> Divided

'Divided, with but half a heart | Till we shall meet'; 'Till we shall meet and never part'. For the reader of such internal secondary codes, it means that these are the persistent left-over feelings of bereavement itself, the simple, tender, but not broken aftermath. So it is that the bereaved poet cries to the grave, to the earth:

> I give thee what I could not keep.
> Be kind to her

The 'give' is like breathing out, letting go; but the 'could not keep' on the same line takes a deep breath back in, by having to admit the other side of the thought of release. The left-over half line that must follow is, again, like the breaking plea of a restrained tear. Without such subtly protective codes and patterns, sentiment would be left exposed or untested, as vulnerable or embarrassing or oppressive. Instead, it is as if in such places literature were something which is at once writing and reading itself, crying and hearing itself, like a live internally communicating reality.

Richards concludes: 'This identification (of = to = for) holds with more poetry and high utterance than we customarily recognize. The speaker becomes a mouthpiece (of = to = for) what speaks, what is communing with itself.'[4] The poet and the poetry *become* what they think of.

The cry in the novel: confession

But the story of the development of this deep aspect of literature has one further twist so great as perhaps to license my introducing it rather simply and obviously. Literature not only bespeaks what too often is not said, or can hardly be said, outside literature. In its evolution it further begins to include within itself the depiction of people *not* doing (even refusing to do) what literature does at the level of expression.

An example would involve turning a novelist imaginatively loose upon all those people in the Sydney street who tried to avoid crying. But here is a different instance, in resistant denial of first things.

A young man knows he is in danger of doing something very wrong. He goes to an older friend, an easy-going clergyman, intent on confessing his temptation in order to prevent it turning into act. But when he gets to his mentor's house, it is not like the old ritual of confession, formally enforcing commitment with the mouth to a hole in the wall and an expectant ear on the other side. The fact that the young man is seated so informally in the presence of an old

friend who has no inkling of the serious internal struggle he has
come to confide, shakes his own belief in the reality of its seriousness. 'It was not, after all, a thing to make a fuss about.' But the
novelist writes:

Was there a motive at work under this strange reluctance of Arthur's which
had a sort of backstairs influence, not admitted to himself? Our mental business is carried on much in the same way as the business of the State: a great
deal of hard work is done by agents who are not acknowledged. In a piece
of machinery, too, I believe there is often a small unnoticeable wheel which
has a great deal to do with the motion of the large obvious ones. Possibly,
there was some such unrecognised agent secretly busy in Arthur's mind at
this moment—possibly it was the fear lest he might hereafter find the fact
of having made a confession to the Rector a serious annoyance, in case
he should *not* be able quite to carry out his good resolutions. (*Adam Bede*,
chapter 16)

Nobody in real life ever wants to be exposed as Arthur Donnithorne
is here by the novel and the novelist around him. In adult life you
can more or less carry on going wrong: often there may be no sign,
no person, no formal procedure to indicate even that it is wrong.
That is how most of us perhaps get by, uneasily let off the hook in
an equivocal version of freedom.

Needing to speak out and yet not wanting to: this is of course one
of those in-between grey areas created by the Victorian novel, in its
depiction of the compromisedness of the ordinary. In the history of
feeling it is that form at that time that most marks out the territory
between the old world and the modern one, a transition that is not
only historical, as if once-and-for-all, but recurrent in every crisis of
modern values.

For of course by a sort of psychological backstairs work, the young
man does succumb to the temptation of the sexual. The young squire
Arthur Donnithorne seduces Hetty, the young woman on his estate
also loved by his woodsman, Adam Bede. When, in chapter 27 entitled
'A Crisis', Adam catches the two of them in an embrace, Arthur
for all his customary self-centredness suddenly experiences that head-
spinning shock so characteristic of the novel's perspectivism—a shock

which made him for the moment see himself in the light of Adam's indignation, and regard Adam's suffering as not merely a consequence, but an ele-

ment of his error. The words of hatred and contempt—the first he had ever heard in his life—seemed like scorching missiles that were making ineffaceable scars on him. All screening self-excuse, which rarely falls quite away while others respect us, forsook him for an instant, and he stood face to face with the first great irrevocable evil he had ever committed.

Suddenly, through this reversal of the normal point of view, there is revealed here a lost and neglected absolute regardless of mitigation or excuse; an ultimate reality disclosed not only to the victim but to the perpetrator, 'face to face' with the 'ineffaceable' and 'irrevocable'. This is the moment of truth revealed by the moment of crisis as it breaks through that 'screen', as George Eliot calls it, of persistent self-excuse which maintains Arthur's ego. It is like the final illness that breaks through the protagonist in Tolstoy's *Death of Ivan Ilyich* to tell him that throughout his life he has not lived as he ought to have lived. And yet, unsurprisingly, Arthur resists this moment which, even because of its pain, could have been the greatest moral moment of his life. Instead, in the middle of the dilemma, he chooses—all too understandably for any reader—evasion and escape, secretly carrying the guilt in preference to openly facing the irrevocable. That is to say: Arthur Donnithorne becomes a second-order person surviving by hiding from 'the first' (a phrase twice used in the passage). He will not occupy the place where the reality most is, where he might actually have to do what the situation requires; he will not let the crisis come to a crisis and break him down into primary confession.

Instead, he feels it is too late and therefore tries, as we say, to get away with it, perhaps also convincing himself of a duty to Hetty's reputation not to let Adam know quite how far beyond kissing they have gone. For at the back of Arthur's mind just before this moment and returning just after it, is a secret thought, the 'small unnoticeable wheel': it is the sly desperation of the get-out clause, like a survival mechanism for the threatened little ego—

Arthur had felt a sudden relief while Adam was speaking; he perceived that Adam had no positive knowledge of the past, and there was no irrevocable damage done by this evening's unfortunate rencontre.

He doesn't know how bad it is. 'There was no irrevocable damage done' as against his previously standing 'face to face with the first

great irrevocable evil he had ever committed': it all depends on
whether we are talking about what Adam knew, or what actually
happened, and how long denial can maintain that screen between
the two. As the psychoanalyst Adam Phillips puts it in his book
On Balance: getting away with it is an uncompleted action, at once
in need and in fear of punishment. For punishment, like crisis,
brings certain acts to their decisive ending: 'It confirms a cause-
and-effect story; it narrows the consequences of actions. [But] if
you get away with it, for however long, you are on the open road
of unpredictable consequence.' These not-having-been-punished
experiences, concludes Phillips, are 'miniature death-of-God experiences', experiments in secret, a desperate privacy radically
defiant of objectivity, when 'you have changed the world without
letting it know'.[5]

In place of confession, then, there is the novel with its discovery
of what is now technically known as 'Free Indirect Discourse': the
inner mental language of the character loosely released, without the
character acknowledging it, into the language of the narrative. The
realist novel does not put 'Arthur thought this or said that'; whatever he thinks, consciously or unconsciously, whatever he does not
say, is simply exposed to sympathy or judgement, to the world of
readers. Free Indirect Discourse restores our second-order evasions
and complications to the verge of direct primary speech in an outer
world.

George Eliot is the best analyst of what she herself also created,
the capacity to move back and forth between those differing powers
in herself, a mark of an extraordinary mental integration. When she
creates the terrible marital row between Lydgate and Rosamond in
Middlemarch, all that she hears unspoken in Lydgate, alone in the
row's aftermath, is a model for her ideal reader's mix of imagination, mitigating sympathy, and utter judgement at almost the self-
same time:

It was as if a fracture in delicate crystal had begun, and he was afraid of
any movement that might make it fatal. His marriage would be a mere
piece of bitter irony if they could not go on loving each other.... She had
still a hold on his heart, and it was his intense desire that the hold should
remain strong. In marriage, the certainty 'She will never love me much', is
easier to bear than the fear, 'I shall love her no more.' (chapter 64)

Neither of those two direct inner voices, '*She* will never love me *much*', '*I* shall love her *no more*', is spoken out loud, is allowed to become the person; though in order to keep going Lydgate tacitly chooses the continuing disappointment of the first to suppress the utter finality of the second. But George Eliot could analyse both of these unspoken utterances as deeply and poignantly as one could any lines of poetry—as indeed she does earlier with Rosamond's response to Lydgate's plea for help: 'What can *I* do, Tertius?'—

That little speech of four words, like so many others in all languages, is capable by varied vocal inflexion of expressing all states of mind from help-less dimness to exhaustive argumentative perception, from the completest self-devoting fellowship to the most neutral aloofness. Rosamond's thin ut-terance threw into the words: 'What can *I* do!' as much neutrality as they could hold. They fell like a mortal chill on Lydgate's roused tenderness. (chapter 58)

That is a great reading as well as a great writing of what lies behind a few little words. It is as it was earlier—not even dramatically 'She will never love me' but 'She will never love me *much*'. That one last little word 'much', like the stressed I in 'What can *I* do?', makes all the difference. Imagining what the characters do not say within what they do, and what they dare not even consciously think, 'George Eliot' exists as such to give a sub-vocal presence to all that goes unvoiced in the world. It is as though unspoken words hang around the characters, like an unadmitted fate into which the reader enters instead, by proxy, to supply unacknowledged thoughts like a character's second and almost unconscious self. From the very inside of her own work George Eliot is the supreme version of that proxy-figure. She *reads* these people as though reading not poetry, but the residue of all ordinary real life.

With George Eliot, wrote the Victorian man of letters John Morley, the reader with a conscience opens the book as though putting him-self in the confessional.[6] Any reluctantly identifying reader possessed of a kindred memory or imagination, an equivalent secret and a conscience, is thus exposed silently as stand-in, in lieu of confession or prayer. All that we have established as upright citizens, all that makes us securely different from the characters gives way in the im-aginative melting-pot of fiction. When a line of poetry strikes with violence, when a character summons sudden terrifying identification, it is as if the thought and the feeling are happening as if for the *first* time again in human life.

'The people who come to evening classes,' says Saul Bellow's Herzog, contemplating his own class, 'are only ostensibly after culture. Their great need is for good sense, clarity, truth—even an atom of it. People are dying—it is no metaphor—for lack of something real to carry home when day is done.'[7]

2. In the middle of things

Ferguson's transitions

In thinking about first things in relation to the midst of things, I take guidance here from a somewhat neglected but historically foundational text, Adam Ferguson's *Essay on the History of Civil Society* (1767). Adam Ferguson was a favourite author of Karl Marx in the development of his theory of alienation, as well as Walter Scott, in his vision of the history of Scotland. His *Essay* is a product of the Scottish Enlightenment yet at the same time challenges the primacy of the Enlightenment ideal of pure rationalism. Its main (we would now say, sociological) purpose was to examine societies in transition from their founding and securing purposes, through both ruptures and accommodations, to later changes and developments in the name of civilization.

In that emergent process it is the creation of separate disciplines and expert practices, says Ferguson, that is crucial to the stabilized improvement and progress of society. But the development of specialist excellence through such division of labour comes at a price. It is the price to be paid when the professionalized separation of each activity reaches the point at which society is composed of highly competent but closed-off parts of which none any longer contains or recalls the spirit needed to animate the whole.

To take an example close to home: it is right, says Ferguson, that libraries are liberally furnished with books, and a citizenry provided with a broad and thorough education. But, he argues, for all the good intentions of improvement there comes a tipping-point when we become passive students instead of creative thinkers and 'substitute the knowledge of books, instead of the inquisitive or animated spirit in which they were written' (part 5, section 3). That is when a society becomes second-order and second-rate, exhausted just at the point when it seems most fair-minded, most reasonably easy-going, and most complete.

Then it is that an unruly minor prophet such as Ferguson is needed, for the purposes of revivification. Ferguson himself was a product of the Scottish Highlands at a time of transition when the rougher, wilder, hotter Highland values were being finally absorbed within the politer commercial mechanisms of the more dispassionately rational Lowlands. The Highlanders, he believed, had been an incorrigibly active and passionate people. They had thrown their passions into their objects—the parent in protection of the child's distress, the citizen in defence of friend or country, with a vehemence of feeling characteristically too strong and too immediate for narrower considerations of personal safety or interest. But as soon as such creatures come to rest in easy economic prosperity, he argued, they decay; courage degenerates into social emulation, while privacy and politeness become smooth civilized alternatives to shared honesty.

Of course, there is an obvious objection to be raised. We are bound to question how far any such sense of something primary that is lost is no more than a backward projection or a nostalgic illusion, at best perhaps a needful rather than an indulgent imagination. But whatever the rights and wrongs of Ferguson's view of human nature—or more aptly, its historical and cultural specifics—what is methodologically instructive is that, even thinking as he did, Ferguson did not seek to go *back* to Highland nature, did not believe he could return to some lost original home furnished with the natural first things of his tribal imagination. What we call 'Nature' was what was happening anywhere at any time, he said, including all the developing arts and inventions of humankind: it was where society was going to, not where it was coming from, that was his concern. Vitally for Ferguson—and this is the great challenge in this chapter—first things are only intuited, realized, tested, superseded, or transformed in the middle of things.

What is more, Ferguson insists that the underlying principles of our energy often flourish in bafflement of human intent, uncoordinated with human recognition. We aim for some end, some peace, some rest, says Ferguson, only to find something else still to be done thereafter; when we obtain the security we think we wanted, we soon take it for granted in seeking something more than that for the sake of life; we are energized by the adversity we do not want. He also believed that the terrible realization of corruption or inertia at the crisis-point of a society's development is often the moment at which, in the realization itself, reform is already actually beginning. In what follows, I relish that excited and not merely sceptical thought of Ferguson's: that, in the mix of the first and the midst, we do not and cannot know wholly where we are or what we are doing.

'A middle state'

In his autobiography *A Sort Of Life*, the novelist Graham Greene talked of his experiencing the memory of his life-story as though through a long broken night. He could not tell the story consecutively, as if he were wide awake and lucid from first to last, but he did feel its presence intermittently surfacing in parts and pieces. 'As I write, it is as though I am waking from sleep continually to grasp at an image which I hope may drag in its wake a whole intact dream, but the fragments remain fragments, the complete story always escapes.'[8] Greene did not feel securely on top of things, but still immersed in their midst. He could take no steady overview of himself but felt instead like some creature working its way intuitively along or within a line of time, with an occasional, temporary sense of loop or return or higher insight en route.

There is a cult novel by E. A. Abbott called *Flatland*, published in 1884 with the sub-title *A Romance in Many Dimensions*, which being made out of a basic geometric template offers a useful model for Greene's sort of experience. In it Abbott imagines a creature living in a two-dimensional plane, the land of the novel's title, who is challenged to ascend to a three-dimensional world, like our own, called Spaceland. The flat creature gets there only by first going down to the lower realm of Lineland and then lower still, to Pointland—both of them closed worlds that can no more imagine a higher dimension, he realizes, than he himself could within the confines of Flatland. By such acts of (as it were) reverse imagination, imagining *less* than he knows now, Abbott's man on his return to Flatland is equivalently impelled, by analogy, to try to 'see' *more* than his own two dimensions tell him. For this is a mind now blindly struggling to think outside its own framework or configuration whilst still embodied within it. It is easy for the creatures in each successive dimension to look down on the level below them and recognize the limitations there: what is harder is to imagine that their own dimension is, likewise and analogously, not the ultimate one. This difficult imagination is what Abbott's protagonist calls Thoughtland. There he tries to hold on to his intimation of an extra dimension by repeating the mantra 'Upwards, and yet not Northwards'—since in his world's terms, northwards would only take him further along existing horizontal lines, not into another dimension above them. He can see it only through the mind's eye, and it is words that he needs to keep a hold on the elusive possibility of that unchartered reality: 'Upwards, and yet not Northwards...I determined steadfastly to retain these words as the clue.' Yet all the time, despite this blind language, he feels his vision of this extra place 'in some strange way slipping away from me, like the image of a half-grasped, tantalizing dream'.[9]

Reading can be like a further prompt or clue in the middle of our long broken night. Its fragments bring out in its readers pieces of their own forgotten experience, or flashes of experiences that had no words or place for themselves, intuitions and half-recognitions that may still remain shadowy, inexplicit, or under-appreciated. It is the openings that matter—the images that almost promise to bring in their wake the whole sub-conscious or unconscious dream.

'I read because I seem to have forgotten so much in life,' a colleague once told me, 'and, even before that, have perhaps under-appreciated or failed to register even more.' Books became a second, added memory. Reading some lines of verse, he thinks as in a burst of involuntary recognition: 'I had forgotten or dismissed something like this; didn't know I needed or had neglected that.' Or even, more blankly: 'I don't know what this is that is somehow affecting me with its not-quite-understood thought, or its strangely reminiscent atmosphere, or its new point-of-view; but it feels like some message that concerns me—without my yet knowing why.'

That mix of half-bafflement and half-enlightenment is what it is like for vulnerably equivocal creatures who are, in the words of Pope at the beginning of the second epistle of his *Essay on Man*, 'placed on this isthmus of a middle state': 'With too much knowledge for the Sceptic side | With too much weakness for the Stoic's pride.' Humans have 'too much' in them for the secondary defences and strategies to be wholly containing or entirely proper; but they also have 'too little' knowledge and 'too little' security for total immunity in the first place.

Awakened and awakening surprise

In that sort of in-between world, neither fully one thing nor another, the simplest course seems to be to try to go on with things—the And then, And then, And then of one thing happening successively after another. 'And we have been on many thousand lines', writes Matthew Arnold in 'The Buried Life', adding, 'But hardly have we, for one little hour, | Been on our own line, have we been ourselves.' We go on and on, says Arnold—

> But often, in the world's most crowded streets
> But often, in the din of strife,
> There rises an unspeakable desire
> After the knowledge of our buried life.

For still, at times, suddenly, and even from within the midst of life, these temporary creatures seek to know 'whence our lives come and where they go'. We want to find the beginning, the purpose, and the destination of the story. It is, of course, a story that may be no more than the fantasy of a lost straight-forwardness, but it still marks a need. And in that need, along that line of time, just sometimes there is a lyric trigger which calls into existence something one did not even know to have been buried:

> A bolt is shot back somewhere in our breast
> And a lost pulse of feeling stirs again.

Arnold puts elegiacally, and perhaps too elegiacally as is his way, what is also electrically exciting—the returned sense of an intermittent or under-used inner life; in the midst of things, a renewed belief in the existence of one's store or reservoir of experience.

There is a single line in Wordsworth that perfectly conveys that deep, almost innocent sense of (what I will call) poetic surprise, which is so often characteristic of the human position within the middle state, whether it occurs inside or outside poetry itself. The experience comes out of a simple evening walk, on Wordsworth's return to the Lake District after an unhappy time in London—a walk made in cold damp circumstances without apparent promise or welcome:

> The sun was set, or setting, when I left
> Our cottage door, and evening soon brought on
> A sober hour, not winning or serene,
> For cold and raw the air was, and untuned;
> But as a face we love is sweetest then
> When sorrow damps it, or, whatever look
> It chance to wear, is sweetest if the heart
> Have fulness in itself; even so with me
> It fared that evening.

This is not verse that needs to *try* to be 'happy': it is what the happiness comes *out of*, the earlier *un*happiness, that is the measure of the value of its happening. For now the poet finds in himself an increasingly gathering calm:

> While on I walked, a comfort seemed to touch
> A heart that had not been disconsolate:
> Strength came where weakness was not known to be,
> At least not felt... (*The Prelude* (1805), 4.142–56)

The great subtle line is, I think, 'Strength came where weakness was not known to be'. The heart had *not* been disconsolate: it is not simply a problem followed by a solution. Deeper and more gently, it is a subtly double experience: he did not know he had previously lacked what now he was glad to be given.

That is the beautiful quality of the coming of surprise, occurring by definition *before* we know it or can know what to make of it. That is when we don't merely use our sense of experience, as though reassuringly in advance, but rather find it. By this I do not mean just any old arbitrarily playful surprise, but surprise into a different state of being. This is why in this section I concentrate on the seriousness of surprise and its variants—intense interest of unexpected attention,

sensitive alertness to unannounced change, bursts of excitement and
semi-recognition, utter wonder—as exemplary of experience, registered suddenly, agnostically, and in passing, in the midst of life.
What matters as the reading goes along is the registering of change,
however minute, even as it happens, and the nascent emotional
charge that accompanies that micro-change even when it is hardly
nameable.

Surprise is therefore, at this level of seriousness, not the vulgar
notion of a one-off novelty but a triggered entry into a different im-
mersive condition. Here, for example, from Thomas Hardy's poem
'Under the Waterfall', is a woman who speaks more gently than
Hardy himself often does, as if not to disturb the domestic atmosphere and what goes on within it:

> Whenever I plunge my arm, like this
> In a basin of water, I never miss
> The sweet sharp sense of a fugitive day
> Fetched back...

It is like a waking dream of the kind that Graham Greene describes,
from the midst of a life. As the hand goes under the water in the
simplest of domestic rituals, the mind by a kind of synaesthesia goes
beneath some equivalent surface-present of its own, feeling around
within itself almost blindly. This is (almost paradoxically) a *regular*
surprise given by her buried life—it cannot stay but it will not go
away. For '*whenever*' she physically plunges her arm in a basin of
water, she repeatedly recalls a glass that her lover and she had al-
ternately drunk from, at a picnic long ago, which she had then tried
to wash in the waterfall:

> Where it slipped, and sank, and was past recall,
> Though we stooped and plumbed the little abyss
> With long bared arms. There the glass still is.

The five last monosyllabic words and their quiet placing in the line
are beautiful in every sense of stillness: 'There the glass still is.' The
woman can't know that for sure, of course. It is an act of imagination and faith that the glass is still there intact, like some pristine
memory preserved elsewhere in the world, which nothing of the
lovers' subsequent story can ever touch or tarnish. The glass hidden

under the waterfall is like the memory now held in the poem. And the immersed hand is like trying to read the experience.

'And, as said, if I thrust my hand below | Cold water in basin or bowl, a throe | From the past awakens that time.' The throe is the spasm, the birth-pang, of thought—the pre-cerebral excitement too often excluded from professionalized accounts of thinking conceived as something inherently dispassionate. But in his *Principles of Psychology* (1855) the evolutionary philosopher Herbert Spencer likened having a thought to receiving a blow—something necessary to be heeded for one's survival. Something hits you, we say still; something strikes you, originally with violence, perhaps in later forms with what Wordsworth called a gentle shock of mild surprise.

There was a boy, wrote Wordsworth, who would playfully mimic the hootings of the owls, that they might answer him; but

> when it chanced
> That pauses of deep silence mocked his skill,
> Then sometimes in that silence, while he hung
> Listening, a gentle shock of mild surprize
> Has carried far into his heart the voice
> Of mountain torrents; or the visible scene
> Would enter unawares into his mind...
> (*The Prelude* (1805), 5.404–10)

It is the unexpected pause and silence in the midst of the game that first make the boyish mind change track. When the young De Quincey came upon these lines, in the company of Wordsworth himself, what he heard most devastatingly within those pauses came from that apparently little word 'far'. This complex scenery, he wrote in *Recollections of the Lakes and the Lake Poets*, has done—What? 'Has carried *far* into his heart the voice | Of mountain torrents'. It always struck him, he says, 'as with a flash of sublime revelation'.[10] In *Creative Evolution* Henri Bergson wrote that sometimes, in the competition for space, life succeeds through having to make itself very small. So here a small passing word opens up everything, as though space itself entered to create the inner world of that boy, re-echoing to the world outside. At that moment De Quincey, feeling like the boy, felt also like a poet.

The example of Douglas Oliver

I first came upon the poet Douglas Oliver at a poetry reading he gave
in Cambridge in 1974 when I was a rather stroppily unhappy and
lonely student, taking a (sort of) evening off from the struggle to read
Milton. Oliver was reading a long poem he had just published, *In The
Cave of Suicession*. It was an account of man called Q, the enquirer,
who in a time of trouble takes himself, some rations, and a typewriter
into a dark abandoned lead mine in the Derbyshire Peak District,
known as Suicide Cave or sometimes Horseshoe Cave. I think Oliver
did say at the time that he had himself done this over many nights for
a period of several months, following the death of his son Tom who,
born with Down's syndrome, had died before his second birthday.
But I do know that I rarely went to poetry readings—disliking (doubtless over-reactively) the often arty atmosphere in which most poets
read their poetry, casually off-hand and down-beat, it seemed to me,
as if they had already done their job in writing it.

Douglas Oliver wasn't like that. When he read aloud, it was
poetry in performance—not performance in the dramatically self-
advertising sense, but something as concentrated, intense, and riskily
present as writing itself repeated in the act of working itself out, the
poet going quietly to the very edge of risk in all the different pitches,
pauses, tempi, and voices he gave himself to. He seemed to know
that if it did not come alive at that moment, the poem was not there
but dead. There is, he said, a vital difference between merely describing an experience and being it or performing it—which is like
the distinction between trying to fix the Truth dogmatically into a
single description and 'half-sensing a perfect truthfulness as a possibility hidden within our actions (performances)'. The latter sense of
truth which is that of the literary way is, he concluded, 'a *non-existent*
entity which nevertheless seems to guide us'.[11]

In Oliver's *Cave* the troubled man named Q spoke and wrote in
the dark, waiting for something called A to answer him back, like an
oracle. But A calmly told Q that he was to write the story of a man
who has acted so badly that he cannot have an oracle. Instead he
must live with his failures constantly reminding him of what he
cannot do, until he can write something good (in every sense) that
is worthy of A. To do so, Q said he understood that he must rid

himself of himself; adding, that he must give up his ambitions for writing some well-polished literary text, but instead retain all the embarrassments and stutters of what he was experiencing there.

I did not understand it properly (probably still do not), and usually I did not appreciate poems like that, so much was I myself wanting answers. Indeed I hated it when people said glibly and preciously that poetry was not something to be understood. But the slow reality and careful authority of the reading from out of the cave made me patient for what seemed even in its quirkiness on the verge of the important. And in retrospect I learnt two things—though in a world that contains such bad models of education, I don't know if 'learnt' is or is not the right word for what comes from such embodied experience.

One was to do with reading aloud—with the way that in one sense it was hardly out loud but rather an external model and an objectified discipline for what could and should go on within, when reading and hearing were most attentively real to a mind taking in the words. Years later, in the late 1990s in Newcastle under Lyme I heard Douglas Oliver read again—in particular a poem entitled 'Well of Sorrows in Purple Tinctures'. In it the poet, now resident in Paris, is walking the night streets, thinking of his English dead ones, of his family—mother, sister, father, and that baby son, Tom. In his mind Oliver also carried the refrain of an old gospel tune, 'life's a burden you can lay down'. The audience kept hearing these two repetitive rhythms in the acoustic world he again created— walking the Paris boulevard, continually walking, with the accents of the deep south in 'lay my burden down, lay my-ah burden down'. Then suddenly this developed from lay my burden down—this quiet and gentle shock:

> See my baby lay his head on a down pillow,
> Pigeons flurrying on the boulevards.
> Lay my bird in down.

My burden...my bird in. It was no trick. He didn't recite his poem; he *made* it again, made it come through itself again, immersed in front of us. Only later, says Oliver, does the performed poem become a 'text' once more, waiting to be re-activated by a reader, silent or aloud.

Thus, the second thing was the sheer *present-ness* of it all. Douglas Oliver was a reader who not only took his time but took the poem's time, like a verbal musician playing live from a text made into score. Latterly, inviting him to Liverpool, I heard him read Hardy or Dryden or Wyatt or Shakespeare or Milton, and it did not matter how long ago it was that the poems were written. He stayed in their time, inside their timing, undistanced from the historical text, as if literature were in that sense and for that moment what is often far too easily called 'timeless'. More accurately, the literature's own internal time, like a form of existence vocally re-created, was for the time the poem lasted, the only time to be registered in reality. It is not that we do not need historical knowledge, historical context to help understand what a text means: it is an important secondary aid. But I have no patience with my university colleague who claimed that no one could read *Paradise Lost* 'properly' without the footnotes in the great Longman's edition plus several books of literary criticism and theological background. Literature is not a branch of history (or politics, or sociology, or philosophy, or theology, or even literary criticism): no one can deny the corrective and informative uses of contextual instruction, but reading literature is time-travel in search of meaning, such that the works of all ages are available as, above all, primary and present.

Milton and Archimedes' lever

Hearing Douglas Oliver was like reading *Paradise Lost* at the moment when Milton's Satan lifts his wings to fly up through Chaos (an abyss that contains all the potential components of the universe), in search of a new world, Earth, which is rumoured to have been created at this time. Then all of a sudden:

> plumb down he drops
> Ten thousand fathom deep, and to this hour
> Down had been falling, had not by ill chance
> The strong rebuff of some tumultuous cloud
> Instinct with fire and nitre hurried him
> As many miles aloft (*Paradise Lost*, 2.933–8)

This is not a fancy sci-fi trip: there is something here about unimaginable origins, long prior to one's own life as a later inhabitant of that once-new planet, still stirring one's memory as though from behind. 'And *to this hour* | Down had been falling': how huge suddenly is Milton's epic and its imagined universe, if all that space took all that time—and the event reaching forward such that Satan could still be falling even now as I read. It feels like some mind-spinning idea in poetic physics, making us take in thoughts we cannot really think. Poetry is often close to that paradox of imagining what is almost inconceivable, where imagination is not so much a simple transcendent triumph as a reflexive product of human limitation recognizing itself.

In the middle of things, without clear starting-points, there are no heroes who can raise the whole world on their own shoulders: we need leverage. Archimedes said that he was capable of building a machine with which he could move the entire earth—if only he could find a place on earth on which to stand it. Literature is a place, close to the impossible, for Archimedes' lever. Wordsworth said that he used the idea of Platonic reminiscence in the 'Immortality Ode'—the idea of an anterior origin or birthright which we dimly recalled in childhood but gradually lost and forgot thereafter—not as something he literally believed in but as an Archimedes lever, employed for the sake of a more shadowy intimation that he had from it. There are tools for the imagination which are less true than the truth that they may help to raise you towards, tools validated only in retrospect by what they riskily enabled. These are the phrases, situations, images that almost promise to bring in their wake the whole sub-conscious dream.

These strong emotions of surprise and excitement in the act of reading do not sit easily with what the philosopher Paul Ricoeur has called the 'hermeneutics of suspicion'. Ricoeur believes that all texts require interpretation in order to find their true meaning; that all interpretation involves suspicion; and that suspicion is occasioned by the gap between the apparent meaning of a text and its real meaning, often to be uncovered in spite of the text's own (frequently subconscious) defences, self-interests, and illusions. But I do not know why thinking and questioning should necessarily take the form of suspicion. Nor do I see why or how sceptical thinking is the place from which we can or should begin. It is a second move, not a first one, and even in second readings I don't want wholly to leave

behind the first responses—as if we now know the poem so well that
we can discount those initial feelings and really begin to criticize it.
The sort of reader I try to encourage in my teaching is one who
starts from curiosity, with potential sympathy, in trying to get into a
text. The first task in the middle of things is to seek to imagine what
is this thing one is reading, and even what it might feel like emotionally to believe what it says.

   Here for example is perhaps one of the most ostensibly conservative passages in English literature—the justification of God in Book
3 of *Paradise Lost*. A modern reader might easily dismiss it, out of
suspicion, protest, or disbelief. But that is not what first happens
when I actually read the lines. Here Milton, most dangerously, has
God Himself speak of how Adam and Eve were created 'sufficient
to have stood though free to fall': theirs was that middle state of
active and passive, when to be created wholly passive would only
make for an automatic obedience which would be no real obedience
at all. They cannot justly accuse me, says Milton's God, that the
fault was in their making, and that their maker could, should and
indeed must have foreseen it—

   As if their predestination overruled
   Their will, disposed by absolute decree
   Of high foreknowledge; they themselves decreed
   Their own revolt, not I: if I foreknew,
   Foreknowledge had no influence on their fault,
   Which had no less proved certain unforeknown. (*Paradise Lost*, 3.114–19)

This is an apologetic argument I would more familiarly understand
if its paradox was unwound in the form of ordinary philosophy or
theology. But the effect here of 'Foreknowledge' at the beginning of
the penultimate line in relation to 'unforeknown' at the end of the
last one—together with 'no influence' and 'no less' in between
them—sets the mind spinning. I could still paraphrase it: it makes
no difference that I, God, could foresee it; the foreseeing is not what
made it happen. But the mysterious effect is still nothing like that
dead paraphrase: in the poetry it is more like the moment that Russell Hoban might call the 'flicker' between one reality and another.
For the lines have almost become different levels of being, and the
thought seems to *be* thought as if for the first time in human life

though coming from above it and translated down into it. The flicker, the great twist-and-turn-around in the lines

> if I foreknew,
> Foreknowledge had no influence on their fault,
> Which had no less proved certain unforeknown.

seems to make that final word and in particular the weight of its first syllable—*un*foreknown—not simply negative but a realization created within and by the language, and almost unextractable from it. At this poetic moment, transcendence is almost mind-burstingly contained within what is transcended; eternity held for a microsecond within the time it also oversees; the large within the small, the law found even in what is surprising. In *Paradise Lost* this thought is made primally alive, because imaginatively that epic is about the first times and their subsequent falling into usage.

'The language-within-language': it's not just 'close reading'

Douglas Oliver died in 2000. Into his critical work *Poetry and Narrative in Performance* (1989) and his autobiographical mix of poetry and prose, *An Island That Is All The World* (1990), went a great deal of a life which he spent investigating the most minute spaces of time, within the lines of verse, almost as if secrets of the temporal universe were modelled or hidden there in those interstices.

Herrick's famous lyric, for example, seems simple, its message of 'seize the day' a conventional enough topos:

> Gather ye rosebuds while ye may,
> Old Time is still a-flying:
> And this same flower that smiles today
> Tomorrow will be dying.

But even here in its opening stanza what makes the little poem more than conventional is the movement between the end of line three ('that smiles *today*') and the beginning of the fourth line ('*Tomorrow* will be dying'). For a fraction of a second—but repeatably so every time you read it—you stay in that otherwise almost uninhabitable middle-most place between 'today' and 'tomorrow' as the one turns into the other so easily. Such a transitional pause between the lines and within the sentence exists in time but, writes Douglas Oliver, 'it also exists outside time in a sort of minor, eternal present, a trembling instant which half stands still, partly resisting the flow of the line which creates it. It probably represents a little model.'[12] '*To*morrow and *to*morrow and *to*morrow,' I once heard Ian McKellen's Macbeth repeat like a chant, 'Creeps in this petty pace from day *to* day | *To*—the last syllable of recorded time': that last 'to' took him over the brink beyond another to-day or any to-morrow.

Herrick's poem begins 'Gather ye rosebuds while ye may', but what it comes to is 'And while ye may, go marry', four stanzas later. That shift of 'while ye may' from the end of one line to the beginning of the other at the poem's close, moves the meaning from threat to motive without changing the words but only their position. As if that were sometimes the only change to temporal facts that we can really make.

That subtle capacity to play off line against sentence is a powerful development of literacy itself. Studies have shown, says the novelist Siri Hustvedt, that the knowledge of the alphabet 'seems to strengthen the ability to understand speech as a series of discrete segments'.[13] You can see words and their formation, not just speak them. Then the creation of clauses in prose, of lines in poetry exponentially increases this capacity to look for meaning, by using more extendedly discrete segments, without losing the temporal sense of the syntactic whole of which they are part.

Such analysis of this language-within-language, of the poetic work done within time, is something now falsely called and impatiently dismissed as old-fashioned 'close reading'—which sounds no better than what myopic old Mr Magoo would do, irritatingly, through pebble glasses. But really it is to do with wanting to know more of how a piece of writing works and see into what that working means—however awkward it is that the time it takes to think it out on paper is so much greater than the time it took for it to happen, so dynamically, in the first place. That is why poetry is itself a much-needed shorthand. Not everything can be fully spelt out, not in the midst of trying to articulate so much. A language-within-language therefore has to say *implicitly* to a reader: 'Take this line with that one', or 'Translate this small thing in passing into a large thing in being', or most often of all 'Ask yourself why this word, this turn, this change is here'. And so it wants to draw the reader into the writerly process, with all its tacit shorthands and signals. Thus it is, for example, when Sir Walter Raleigh writes on his loss and his folly in affairs of the heart:

> With wisdom's eyes had but blind fortune seen
> Then had my love, my love for ever been.

The poem at this point innerly says: Feel in the middle of the last line the forward reading-movement become also for the moment a movement back, the language-within-language still secretly crying from its heart, 'my love, my love', like an extra clause created between the two.

This is more than just the learning of something of the writer's trade secrets (as here, in Raleigh, the rhetorical figure of epizeuxis, for example), where technique would be offered as a merely persuasive means to the communication of a definite end. As I have tried to demonstrate, the very processes of making and finding meaning are more intimately shared between careful writers and sympathetic readers than that account allows, and the language-within-language is itself crucial to that realized meaning. For Wordsworth, indeed, there was no part of the poet's craft that didn't turn into something human as he worked with it: the underlying rhythmic heart-beat of a poem was not just a matter for a learned expert in the variety of metres but the pulsating co-presence of something regular to support the irregular feelings above it, like a steadily varying ground on which to keep walking and thinking. To register such hidden inner meanings of the art is not, then, simply a specialist skill for a creative-writing course, or for a university degree in literature: it is a craft of reading and re-reading for any serious reader who needs to slow and stop, to understand more of the feeling, when something along the lines or the sentences suddenly and arrestingly matters.

In Cambridge, in the founding of literary studies in the 1920s and 1930s by I. A. Richards, Mansfield Forbes, and F. R. Leavis, close reading had been known as Practical Criticism. It is more the word 'practical' than the word 'criticism' I want to hold on to. For what is involved is reading in practice or in action, when the reader, attentively following a journey to meaning through line and sentence, is sensitized even to the ostensibly small and passing. Practical Criticism was meant to be what we actually *do* when we read slowly, immersed in the midst of things, conscious of their syntactic twists and turns— not what we *say* we do, before or after the experience.

And herein lies the importance of the difference between what in Aristotle is known as *praxis* as compared with *technē*. *Technē* is what you get if you read a car manual. The manual teaches you the mechanics. You follow the instructions and you can repeat what it tells you: that's technique. Reading self-help books sometimes feels like this: how to cure your depression—step one...But *praxis* as in practical criticism isn't like that. *Praxis* has to do with what you cannot simply be told in advance or in theory; it is to do with abilities that you learn and accumulate in practice. Technique is programmed: crucially, it never adjusts. But the practice of reading does adjust to what is unpredictable, when reading easily and successively left-to-right has to give way, without announcement, to an alert openness, to surprise en route, even in the very midst of a sentence. Skills-based reading in schools is technē: it requires teachers to provide a do-it-yourself tool-kit of blunt instruments—trace the images, find the themes, research a bit of historical context.

Relatively unprogrammed, venturesome reading is attentive to what goes on inside a process without clear principles to start from or a destination easily in sight. (That is why *Flatland* is a great guide to what it feels like in working along the lines.) Such is the nature of a praxis. According to the eighteenth-century visionary philosopher Vico, these practices are the most genuine and reliable knowing that human beings have: we know most from what we have made and from what we have done, *in* the doing and *in* the making—so here, in the course of the writing and in the reading that follows its traces.[14] We have all these large nouns with large expectations attached to them—such as hope, love, faith. But in *Four Quartets*, 'East Coker', T. S. Eliot austerely says it is necessary to wait without these things when they are too large, too prematurely needed, too direct; but the faith, and the hope, and the love, he writes, are 'all *in* the waiting'.

And of course, if this patiently excited immersion in process is an effect of poetry, I do not mean to suggest that the poetry suddenly realized in its journey does not go on in prose, in fiction too. I can think of a hundred examples of this surprise and discovery amidst the apparently prosaic, but two bare, little, yet austerely mind-spinning instances may briefly serve.

In Graham Swift's novel *Wish You Were Here* (2011), there's a middle-aged man called Jack Luxton who is staring at a blank newspaper photograph of his younger brother Tom, killed in active service in Iran. The bereaved man finds himself wanting some 'indication in the face' that Tom might have known, at the time the photo had been taken, that one day his brother would look at it, as Jack does now intently. But (of course) there is no such sign, there never is in the world.

Or, three friends walk along the evening shore together in calm happiness at the close of Stanley Middleton's *Toward the Sea* (1995), wondering casually where they will all be in three years' time. The novel for a minute flashes forward to that future date, when in fact they will no longer be together, and then flashes back again, without irony, to their all still thinking this to have been a wonderful and unforgettable evening.

Necessarily, these two strange but recognizable moments at the macro-level of human story are accompanied and created by quietly equivalent verbal surprises at the micro-level. In Swift: 'And the expression was—expressionless'; in Middleton: 'and they walked on. In ignorance.' These non-happenings are, as it were, the impossible and unpotentiated shifts for people living along in time, below a metaphysical perspective they may suspect but cannot attain, in a kind of Flatland.

Original thinking

But there is a larger point to be made concerning Herrick and the novelists on the theme of time passing, or Milton and the novelists on freewill in the retrospective light of the future. What matters here is the way in which these chosen episodes are and are not 'original' thoughts. As a teacher nothing is much worse for me than when students are discouraged to find something they have read or have thought is already known and catalogued beforehand. It's a commonplace 'topos' in Elizabethan poetry, someone will helpfully tell them. Or they themselves will find in the secondary reading called research some critic who they think has already had 'their idea' far better than they ever will. (And so, in turn, the range of Ph.D. topics narrows, in desperation for a new angle or niche, and there are perfectly intelligent young scholars encouraged to research into matter such as 'the imperialism of mahogany furniture in the novels of Charles Dickens'.)

It should not matter if a thought has been thought before: for the sake of their courage and their confidence the students need to know that it does not matter who previously may have had their idea, so long as this time the thoughts do indeed originate with themselves. To each his or her own realization. It should not be as it is with Hardy's Tess, afraid to study history:

> what's the use of learning that I am one of a long row only—finding out that there is set down in some old book, somebody just like me, and to know that I shall only act her part; making me sad, that's all. The best is not to remember that your nature and your past doings have been like thousands' and thousands', and that your coming life and doings'll be like thousands' and thousands'. (*Tess of the d'Urbervilles*, chapter 14)

That is the plight of passivity to the point of anonymity. It is like reading gone wrong: the power of identification turned into the diminishing and pre-emptive sense of mere biological repetition.

Literary-minded thinkers will not want to be repetitively formulaic, but the alternative is not that they have to be constantly concerned with novelty: writers needn't be, readers shouldn't have to be. That does not mean that all that literature has to offer is 'style', an ornamental way of dressing things up. That precisely is *not* what Pope meant when in his *Essay on Criticism* he wrote of 'what oft was thought, but ne'er so well expressed'. The poet there is rather the great representative, the reflective heightener of what is common: 'Something, whose truth convinced at sight we find | That gives us back the image of our mind' (298–300). And there remains something of Pope's Augustan sense of commonality in Wordsworth himself, for all his quarrel with Pope's diction.

For to Wordsworth an original thought is above all a thought that goes back to the origins of its thinking, to the deepest place it can come from, whether that thought seems apparently new or ostensibly familiar. Thinking about epitaphs, that primal mortal writing of marks inscribed on the permanence of stone and left to the bare external elements of the world, Wordsworth concludes that they should contain thoughts and feelings which are commonplace, rather than fancily poetic or idiosyncratic, because fundamentally epitaphs belong to a universal human story from birth to death. But even with epitaphs, he goes on:

> it is required that these truths should be instinctively ejaculated or should rise irresistibly from circumstances; in a word that they should be uttered in such connection as shall make it felt that they are not adopted, not spoken by rote, but perceived in their whole compass with the freshness and clearness of an original intuition. The Writer must introduce the truth with such accompaniment as shall imply that he has mounted to the sources of things, penetrated the dark cavern from which the river that murmurs in every one's ear has flowed from generation to generation.[15]

Yet unlike epitaphs, Poetry cannot afford its subjects to be taken for granted, when what it speaks for is so often unable to take care of itself. That is why for Wordsworth poetry is like a *second* form of epitaph, a stronger and more individual verbal defence for the sake of the memories it seeks to create, support, and preserve. But in both poetry and epitaph, it is still the source of things that he wants to include even in the midst of things, 'the freshness and clearness of an original intuition'. It does not matter if what is written has been thought before: at the moment of articulation the thought is sheerly in the present tense, brought to life as for the first time. Being that comes *before* knowing, the realization of an ontology ahead of any epistemology that arises out of it: that is the priority here.

What is therefore wonderful about the examples and instances I have cited, and what makes them original again in Wordsworth's sense, is that they all seem to be configured so as to make their words seem called for, coming therefore at the *right* time—when they are newly meant because really needed. It is like the epitaphic speech near the end of *Macbeth* when the wearied, beaten protagonist seems to be as much hearing, as speaking, his own report:

> My way of life
> Is fallen into the sere, the yellow leaf,
> And that which should accompany old age,
> As honour, love, obedience, troops of friends
> I must not look to have . . . (5.3.24–8)

When you read it well, out loud, it feels as though you have almost to *wait* for the right instant to add, across the line, that belated, stranded, and inevitable blow—'I must not look to have'. En route to it, in that killingly slow list, the man feels all over again the meaning of what he once more loses in the naming of it. Like death, that delayed main verbal clause ('I must not look to have') is bound to come; but it also hangs there in what Douglas Oliver called a minor eternal present, out of the resolution of which a lifetime is won or lost on the earth.

In literature and in thinking about literature, what is great is when thoughts—even terrible thoughts—seem triggered by the feel of the sheer situation that is amassing. Then they feel called for, mandated by the moment, when more usually in the cool climate of notional existence intelligence offers what seems only plausible rather than urgently necessary, and our thoughts can feel arbitrary or neglected. But poetic-like occasions are what thought truly exists *for*, as William James describes in *The Varieties of Religious Experience*:

We have a thought, or we perform an act, repeatedly, but on a certain day the real meaning of the thought peals through us for the first time, or the act has suddenly turned into a moral impossibility. All we know is that there are dead feelings, dead ideas, and cold beliefs, and there are hot and live ones; and when one grows hot and alive within us, everything has to recrystallize about it. (Lecture 9 'Conversion')

These hot spots suddenly become centres of redirected energy and, out of that gathering, centres of a relocated self. They are, says James, models of new realization—creating inner constellations of freshly re-configured thoughts, rapid shifts of energy or gravity to these new centres. In literature we have the privilege of seeing these thoughts forming and re-forming themselves, through their verbal forms and syntactic pathways.

What is mortally heartening, moreover, is James's sense of the continuity of such moments with more ordinary occurrences of change. He writes: 'Our ordinary alterations of character as we pass from one of our aims to another are not commonly called transformations, because each of them is so rapidly succeeded by another in the reverse direction.' But these small, common movements of emotional alternation are the neural foundation for a larger transformation if a suddenly created centre becomes magnetically powerful. Further, they are the basis for the experience of radical conversion if that centre expels definitively its rivals and alternatives.

Consider, in this light, the great fifth-act change, the slowed reconciliation of mind finally achieved by a Hamlet no longer at the mercy of what will happen to him. There is nothing here in any single one of these three or four prose sentences that seems particularly 'original', at the level of novelty:

> If it be now, 'tis not to come. If it be not to come, it will be now. If it be not now, yet it will come. The readiness is all.

This is not static thought, the sort you can apply at any time; but thought in motion summoned at a critical stage in a life. As a reader you cannot therefore easily put your finger on it, and yet somewhere in the midst of reading-in-time, the whole (or 'all') becomes far more than its several parts (each 'not'). It is as if what is successive in time can be existent simultaneously at some higher level of thought. This is what the unexceptional characters in Graham Swift or Stanley Middleton could not attain. But what Douglas Oliver wrote of some lines from *The Merchant of Venice* applies equally in the case of this speech of Hamlet's: 'Once or twice in my life, I have read these lines to myself and discovered a strange sliding sensation in my consciousness.' It is fashionable to talk, after Csikszentmihalyi, of being in 'the flow', the thick of concentrated experience, but in its sliding this poetic language *is* the flow in the midst of life: If it be now/'tis not to come; if it be not to come/it will be now; if it be not now/yet it will come. These lines about time take their own time now, for at each rhythmic pause or stress, as Douglas Oliver puts it, there is

> a temporal glide in my mind, as if I had extra time to choose when to pronounce a vowel or a consonant or decide a duration. It makes me feel how immensely gifted and versatile poetically I *could* be, although it is really Shakespeare who has placed that potential in me.[16]

'I must not look to have', 'Yet it *will* come.' In the readiness of all, the words themselves seem ready when they do come. There is not just a character here, a Macbeth or Hamlet, but a mind created on the page, working out where that character now is in the realms of life. And so-called close reading is like a probe trying equivalently to work out the unspoken and unspeakable movements of the stimulated brain-work that underlyingly enables the meaning. 'Thought in its dumb cradles' as Shakespeare himself calls it in *Troilus and Cressida* (3.3.193).

Too easily dismissed as old-fashioned nit-picking, or a practice too naively unsuspicious without theory and knowledge to support it, such reading *is* a version of brain-imaging, as argued in Chapter 1, is the humanities' mind-and-brain science. The apparently small things with which this reading is concerned—a word-shift here, an infinitesimal pause there—are really big things happening at such an unavoidably transient pace as makes them hard even to talk or think about. But they need to be, for that very reason. To put it another way, reading intently is like 'creative writing' done the other way round: not going forward from tacit mentality into the making of words but working backward from the making of words into the mentality implicit within, behind, and beneath them. Reading-in-the-midst of things is the great venture for making out meaning in its very happening.

3. Realizations

Literature, and the thinking that comes out of literature, can only *do* its work, without those guaranteed safeguards or secure foundations it can solely find in the doing. In the creative world in which reading involves us, from the midst of things as I have said, there is less time for knowing in advance, less room for having set opinions and pre-arranged categories. Investigative readers, like writers, need to keep as close as they can to their blind nerves, to the deep internal instincts that seem triggered by the immersion in books, quite before any arrival at a fuller, more familiar sense of their meaning. The best work is thus done not at macro-level from top-down, but as Oliver Sacks describes it, by 'sudden ascents from one level to the next, each level inconceivable to the level below'.[17]

That is not to say, however, that in this literary *ethos*, as I have called it, there is no place for beliefs but only non-committal possibilities instead. Granted: in the crucible of the work, beliefs and intentions and plans and foreseeings must as far as it is possible *not* be imposed; they have to re-emerge, to re-assemble themselves in dynamic memory, to be *realized* again (in both senses of that word) through the tests and calls of a specific situation. But without them, and without the opportunity for emotional discovery, it's the post-modern game of playing around among possibilities none of which actually matters.

Ruskin's help: on realizing the whole

To conclude, I turn to another of those primitive aboriginal human oaks, the Victorian art critic and social thinker John Ruskin. In particular I am thinking of an important moment that occurs oddly but characteristically in a long footnote towards the end of the fifth and final volume of *Modern Painters* (1860), as though he hardly knew where to put an incidental thought that actually took an overview of his work.

In this footnote, looking back across his writings on art as a whole, Ruskin reports how he has often found himself saying several apparently contradictory or ill-fitting things, all of which seem to him separately true, only in different contexts or at different times. Actually, the thought-provoking, simmering messiness of his work rather delighted him, as a trustworthy alternative to the lifelessness of boringly predictable and repeated consistency. It felt analogous to the situation of his beloved Turner on varnishing day immediately before the opening of the Royal Academy exhibition, when only at the very last moment, he would interconnect all the scattered and indistinct parts of his painting, and bring the whole into light with one final touch. Writes Ruskin:

I do not wonder at people sometimes thinking I contradict myself when they come suddenly on any of the scattered passages, in which I was forced to insist on the opposite practical applications of subtle principles.

And yet all these apparently contradictory passages, says Ruskin with great defiant gusto, are perfectly accurate and just:

The essential thing for the reader is to receive their truth, however little he may be able to see their consistency. If truths of apparently contrary character are candidly and rightly received, they will fit themselves together in the mind without any trouble. (*Modern Painters*, vol. v part 9, chapter 7, footnote to para. 23)

Ruskin trusts the awkward differences between the contradictory thoughts that arise on different occasions, on the grounds that such independent realities are proof that he hasn't set them all up together, through some temptation to force a fictively unified consistency. Receive the truths *before* you look for their consistency, he urges in his unapologetic didacticism: otherwise you will never see anything that is not immediately consistent with what you already think. It is the order of things that matters, and it is not an abstract logical order. Only *after* you have received the several truths, will they then *fit themselves* together if indeed they are substantially true. Brought together in mind, it will be as though the combined and contending energy of these several ideas will of itself call forth the thought and the syntax that may rightly connect them.

That is to say: you don't have to go into every situation trying consciously to 'remember' what your principles are, for that would mean they were not really principles. And certainly not principles that are indeed 'subtle' in that deep sense to which Ruskin refers. Subtle principles are not simply definable, are not narrow statements of intent, but are lodged as working orientations within and beneath your actions and your passions and your praxis. In an awakened ontology and an honourable ethos, principle and knowledge are like events which return, I have argued, as if happening for the first time again: the painting, the mountain, the cathedral, the great idea, seen at the right distance, suddenly gathers itself and raises its weight into a whole. This sudden integration feels less like a top-down directive than the creation and re-creation of the materials of life from below upwards, from founding sources.

In *The Naïve and Sentimental Novelist* (2011) Orhan Pamuk offers the belief that even as they go along in time as horizontal linear narratives, novels have hidden within their architecture a secret inner centre, a hiddenly connecting keystone, for which readers must seek. It may be the coalescing moment in Dickens's *Bleak House* when suddenly after 700 pages, the novel's deep emotional centre re-emerges in of all unlikely places, the hitherto effete old aristocrat, Sir Leicester Dedlock, made paralyzed by his wife's guilty desertion: 'After vainly trying to make himself known in speech, he makes signs for a pencil.... Sir Leicester writes upon the slate, "Full

forgiveness".' Or it may rest in what is generated in the space between the characters in *Great Expectations*: Biddy asking Pip, when he
says how unsuitable his new upper-class life will be to lowly Joe
Gargery, the man who has looked out for him all his previous life:
'Don't you think he knows that?' Alternatively the centre may lie in
what *never* happens—between Lydgate and Dorothea in *Middlemarch*, or Levin and Anna in *Anna Karenina*. Or in an idea that could
pass for incidental detail but isn't, like Conrad's MacWhirr relieved
to find a little box of matches in the place they should be even at
the height of the typhoon. Such things are like the very end of
Virginia Woolf's *To the Lighthouse*, when the painter Lily Briscoe
suddenly finishes her picture with a single stroke, drawing 'a line
there, in the centre'.

It isn't just novels that thus gather and disclose themselves from
the midst of within. A play such as *As You Like It* gradually forms and
then finally reveals the centre of its own network. Rosalind, disguised as the young man Ganymede, has been saying to her would-
be beloved Orlando, again and again, to this effect: 'What if I *were*
the Rosalind you love? Pretend I am: suppose I am. Can't you still
think of me as her?' To which Orlando finally and magnificently
bursts out, like an anti-Hamlet:

> I can live no longer by thinking. (5.2.50)

It is no thoughtless affirmation; it is the force of life itself speaking
through him on behalf of the deepest meaning of Shakespearean
comedy. This too is Dickens's model: that a character will erupt out
of the dense medium of the crowded novel momentarily to claim
and gather together the whole. And if not, then the character, like
Barnardine in *Measure of Measure*, may decline to fit his life conveniently to the plot, insisting that somewhere still the part can be defi-
antly more than the whole: 'I swear I will not die today, for any
man's persuasion' (4.3.56). In Dickens, particularly the later Dickens
from *Little Dorrit* onwards, the whole is then re-created anew when
the character finds he or she cannot be wholly free but is tied to a
larger ramifying society. Or when the network of that novel silently
asks its reader morally to compare, via Clennam who knows them
both, the false artist Henry Gowan with the great engineer Daniel
Doyce.

The structural dynamic here has to do with the pattern Ruskin describes in one of his prefaces. Generalization as commonly understood is, he asserts in all the joy of his aggression, 'the act of a vulgar, incapable, and unthinking mind':

To see in all mountains nothing but similar heaps of earth; in all rocks, nothing but similar concretions of solid matter; in all trees, nothing but similar accumulations of leaves, is no sign of high feeling or extended thought. The more we know and the more we feel, the more we separate...

But, he goes on, significantly, to a second move:

we separate to obtain a more perfect unity. Stones, in the thoughts of the peasant, lie as they do on his field; one is like another, and there is no connection between any of them. The geologist distinguishes, and in distinguishing connects them. Each becomes different from his fellow, but in differing from, forms a relation to, his fellow; they are no more each the repetition of the other, they are parts of a system; and each implies and is connected with the existence of the rest.[18]

That is what makes a true generalization—when Ruskin follows Wordsworth (in the great 'Preface to Lyrical Ballads') in recognizing the perception of dissimilitude in similitude, of similitude in dissimilitude as the great reproductive principle of life itself. No sameness without difference, but no difference without sameness; no repetition without variation and vice versa: this is the law of creation and re-creation. It is what makes for what Wordsworth calls 'connections finer than those of contrast', as in the generation of an underlying syntax by which 'each in differing from, forms a relation to, his fellow'. That is how suddenly in the life of a novel, a drama, or a poem, parts cry to other parts across their distance, characters call to each other through their diversity, a movement in one place creates another separate shift elsewhere, and books themselves find readers through the compelling mixture of their likeness and their difference.

Ruskin's help again: on the medium of paint

Only interested in the great fundamentals but willing to seek for them through the density of minute particulars, Ruskin was just as capable as was Tolstoy of daring to write a book called *What*

Is Art? For Ruskin, art meant above all painting, though painting made him a great writer. And before I end this chapter with an attempt at some literary conclusions, I want to travel with Ruskin across the disciplines into his own chosen art-form because, as I shall argue in Chapter 3, it is important to go away before returning home.

Ruskin puritanically hated establishment 'Art' with a capital A: meaning, an artificially specialized second-order activity, self-contained and self-sustaining, which allowed a painter to produce a perfectly 'good' painting without ever having to enquire into art's original purpose. He loathed it when a painter over-filled the space and too-completely 'finished' his painting. This was getting in the way of the imagination as his beloved Turner never did in the suggestiveness of his brush-strokes. 'You are coming *between* me and nature,' Ruskin would want to cry impatiently to the over-precise, over-picturesque professional:

He is like a dull story-teller, dwelling on points which the hearer anticipates or disregards. The imagination will say to him: 'I knew all that before; I don't want to be told that. Go on; or be silent, and let me go on in my own way.'

It may sound like a paradox for one who so vehemently claimed not to be an aesthete, but precisely for that reason what Ruskin needed was to *see* that a painting was confessedly a *painting*—not an ostensibly transparent, overly professionalized picture presented like a painted window on the world to be passively looked through; but art as a trigger for imaginative vision. He knew it was indeed art-as-imagination, when he looked at Turner's 'Snow-Storm: Steamboat off a Harbour's Mouth'—it was like looking into the very eye of the storm, at the centre of which the ship is helplessly trapped amidst an intermingled turmoil of indistinguishable sea and sky. Yet when he closely examined the whole surface all he could see were the violent obtrusive sweeps and marks of the brush, black paint flecked with white wildly in an immense confusion:

a good painter is obliged, working near his picture, to do in everything only about half of what he wants, the rest being done by the distance.... Hence the amazement and blank wonder of the public at some of the finest passages of Turner, which look like a mere meaningless and disorderly work of

chance: but rightly understood, are preparations for a given result, like the
most subtle moves of a game of chess, of which no by-stander can for a long
time see the intention, but which are, in dim, underhand, wonderful way,
bringing out their foreseen and inevitable result. (*Modern Painters*, vol. iv,
chapter 4, paragraph 14)

That is to say: when, as the painter's light urged him, Ruskin stared
into the centre of it all, suddenly the picture *happened*, was transformed. A seemingly less material dimension was created out of the
very materials of two-dimensional suggestion, and the whole came
to life. The brush-strokes, without ever appearing to be any less
brush-strokes, changed into meaning, into sea and sky and air and
water whipped into one, became a painting. And that was the
moment of visual realization to Ruskin, when paint and imagination
crossed over, when the mere brush-stroke and what it was meant to
represent flickered to and fro, as if disclosing the secret origin of art
itself by the smallest and slenderest of possible means:

The more subtle the power of the artist, the more curious the difference will
be between the apparent means and the effect produced. (*Modern Painters*,
vol. iv, chapter 4, paragraph 15)

Turner had made his painting work like that by not over-polishing
it, by undisguisedly exposing the apparent means instead—making
the rough and imperfect flicker of paint itself part of the extended
language:

Everything imperfectly realised (as, for instance, by a mere outline of a tree)
necessarily makes us think not only of the thing itself, but of the sort of
stroke or mark which represents it. If art were perfect, it could not be dis-
tinguished from the reality.[19]

But it is important for Ruskin that art is not simply identical with
the reality:

Painting has its peculiar virtues, not only consistent with, but even resulting
from, its shortcomings and weaknesses. (*Modern Painters*, vol. iii, chapter 10,
paragraph 7)

This again is art's language-within-language that implicitly says as
it were, 'I am a painting—which is to say: I am a human effort

within painting that uses paint to try to signal something beyond painting.'

Such tacit cross-over messages from within a work remain in touch with the origins of art. The archaeologist Steven Mithen talks of the discovery of artefacts from the prehistory of art: 'A shell was also a bead. A piece of wood was also a musical instrument. Charcoal and ochre marks on a wall were also a rhinoceros.'[20] No wonder then, we might conclude, that metaphor seems so close to something crucial to art when art's very instruments are at once themselves *and* something else, flickering between the two.

What in literature are the equivalent of those marks on the wall, those distinct brush-strokes, or that visible process of amazingly shared transformation from one thing into another?

Examples of literature's place of awakening

Here are my two final examples, in answer: from a novel and from a poem-sequence.

In Graham Swift's *Wish You Were Here,* Jack Luxton is an unexceptionally lost and baffled man who does not speak much and is not very used to his own thoughts. Yet, supposing himself to be on the verge of suicide, he remembers without apparent reason a regular journey he would make with the family dog in the back of the pick-up to see the girlfriend who was to become, somewhat unhappily at times, his future wife.

We have already read of this trip of young excitement 200 pages earlier. But now it comes back and Jack realizes, oddly, that at the time he had not known—and of course, could not possibly have known—that the memory of 'his doing just what he was doing' at that time might turn out to be 'one of his last thoughts'. Even so, he also recalls that that same dog when aged and sick had seemed to know in advance, for just a split-second, that Jack's father, the old farmer, was going to have to shoot him. At the very last moment, Jack recalls without certainty, the dog had perhaps very slightly lowered his head.

At any rate, by one of those strange loops of time that Thomas Hardy knew so well, something that existed unremarkably in its own

right, a journey with a still lively dog, returns at a different level to
signify—what? not quite a symbol but whatever it is that a lifetime
means. Its coming back has turned it into an inarticulate man's
dumb second language, a brush-stroke with which to paint a miniature. Even in this austere minimalism, what Graham Swift gently
offers is the peculiar experience of reality-shifts, a flicker to-and-fro,
the sensation of a familiar pattern surfacing through strangeness. A
little word here or there, and it is like a poetry bringing the novel
together.

My second example is poetry, conversely, from a sequence that is
like a story from a novel. An unattractive and sickly woman suddenly finds herself loving and beloved, when she had long given up
any such hope. It is not a straightforward narrative: being as it is
almost too good to be true, too wonderful to bear, too painfully new
to be realized, she cannot simply and immediately accept this love
with the delight she knows she should. Elizabeth Barrett Browning
needs poetry to manage and to trust her own extraordinary transition into unexpected happiness. Love is beautiful, she writes, though
I myself am not, and

> when I say at need
> *I love thee*...mark...*I love thee*—in thy sight
> I stand transfigured, glorified aright,
> With conscience of the new rays that proceed
> Out of my face towards thine....
> And what I *feel*, across the inferior features
> Of what I *am*, doth flash itself
>   ('Sonnets from the Portuguese', 10)

There are in this verse two beautiful little models, two fine images,
of poetry itself.

One is to do with how poetry is achieved near the very boundary
of human limitation, when (as Ruskin suggests) limitation is precisely the trigger for imagination. Here the woman is naturally
limited by being bound inside herself (she is physically a separate
self, who cannot see her own face), and limited again psychologically by her inner sense of herself as outwardly plain. The poem
comes out of her knowing her own face to be transformed by her
sight of *his* looking at her love for him. That is poetry on the mind-
spinning verge of the impossible—which is what it seems here. The

woman only knows what she has given out by receiving it back, with gratitude.

The other is to do with the words, like brush-strokes, in the flicker of an instant turning into what they stand for, without ever ceasing to be themselves. I say 'I love thee'—and—(I do) '*I love thee*'. In its visible textuality, it is in its own way like Hopkins in 'Carrion Comfort' saying finally, in terror: 'I wretch lay wrestling with (my God!) my God'. That first '(my God!)' in Hopkins and that second 'I love thee' in Barrett Browning are language-within-language: a second language raised upon and realized through the first until it reaches the fullest out-burst of its own meaning. It is then that the words are not just something within the separate realm of art, merely left to themselves inside a poem. They have found and created a special space for their meaning on the almost impossible boundary between two realms, like Turner's still present brush-strokes. Literary language summons the presence of what it refers to. And the words that have most present reality, created on the back of other words— (my God!); *I love thee*—lift themselves so as actually to exist in that realm *between* art and life which art itself exists to create.

Or to put it more simply, through the resonant brevity of art again. In what poses as a children's book, one of Russell Hoban's heroes, required to handle a task too big for him, feels he has been mistaken for a shaman when really he is but a shamed man. During his strange quest, as a bad man seeking to do one final good thing, he asks his mentor what realm is he in: whether he is alive or dead, whether he is awake or still living within his dream. I don't know, she replies, 'But I don't think it makes any difference, you just have to face it however it comes to you.'[21]

That is when the fictional becomes real.

Notes

1. William James, *Varieties of Religious Experience*, first published 1902 (Harmondsworth: Penguin, 1985), 186.
2. I am indebted to Catherine Pickstock for the term in her *After Writing* (Oxford: Blackwell, 1998).
3. Kenelm Digby, *Two Treatises* (1644), quoted in John L. Russell, 'Action and Reaction Before Newton', *British Journal for the History of Science* 9 (1976), 25–38.

4. I. A. Richards, *Beyond* (New York: Harcourt, 1974), 95–6.

5. Adam Phillips, *On Balance* (London: Hamish Hamilton, 2010), 205.

6. John Morley, *Nineteenth-Century Essays*, ed. Peter Stansky (Chicago: University of Chicago Press, 1970), 309 ('The Life of George Eliot' also reprinted in Morley's *Critical Miscellanies* (1888), vol. iii).

7. Saul Bellow, *Herzog* (Harmondsworth: Penguin, 1965), 34.

8. Graham Greene, *A Sort of Life* (Harmondsworth: Penguin, 1974), 25.

9. *Flatland: A Romance of Many Dimensions* (London: Penguin, 1998), 107, 112.

10. Thomas De Quincey, *Recollections of the Lakes and the Lake Poets* (1834–40), ed. David Wright (Harmondsworth: Penguin, 1970), 161.

11. Letter to Anselm Berrigan: <http://www.poetryfoundation.org/harriet/2009/10/poetry-and-narrative-in-performance-part-i/>.

12. Douglas Oliver, *Poetry and Narrative in Performance* (Basingstoke: Macmillan, 1989), 19.

13. Siri Hustvedt, *Living, Thinking, Looking* (London: Sceptre, 2012), 133 ('On Reading').

14. Isaiah Berlin, *Vico and Herder* (London: Hogarth Press, 1978), 122.

15. *The Prose Works of William Wordsworth*, ed. W. J. B. Owen and Jane Worthington Smyser, 3 vols. (Oxford: Oxford University Press, 1974), ii. 78–9.

16. Oliver, *Poetry and Narrative in Performance*, 82.

17. Oliver Sacks, *A Leg to Stand On* (London: Picador, 1986), 141.

18. John Ruskin, *Selelcted Writings*, ed. Philip Davis (London: Everyman, J. M. Dent, 1995), 45 (to be found in E. T. Cook and Alexander Wedderburn (eds.), *Library Edition of the Works of John Ruskin* (London: George Allen, 1903–12), iii. 7–8).

19. Ruskin, *Selected Writings*, 114–15 (Cook and Wedderburn, *Library Edition*, vii. 358–60).

20. I am indebted here to Keith Oatley, *Such Stuff as Dreams* (Chichester: Wiley-Blackwell, 2011), 29.

21. Russell Hoban, *Soonchild* (London: Walker Books, 2012), 51.

3

The Holding-Ground and the World

Introduction

The achievement of movements

At the very last moment in the sacrifice of Isaac, an angel of the Lord intercedes to stop Abraham as he raises the knife, and substitute a ram in place of his son. This starkly externalized ancient narrative is, as one great reader has put it, 'fraught with background', but it is a background left unexpressed—the thoughts, feelings, and motivation behind the austere authority of the bare history only suggested by the silence amidst the fragmentary speeches.[1] In his imaginative back-filling of the biblical text, what especially amazed Kierkegaard was Abraham's instant reaction to this sudden release of Isaac. Abraham seems to receive his son back with an immediate forgetfulness of all he has been forced to go through and with an instantly heart-felt joy. He needed no time to come to terms with the relief, says Kierkegaard, no transitional preparation to return from the realm of the infinite and the absolute, back down again to the common land of finitude. Kierkegaard confesses that for himself he could never have made that sudden shift in one pure go, without resentment for the past. It would have taken him at least two mental movements to readjust to the sudden present:

I could easily fill a whole book with the various misunderstandings, awkward positions, and slovenly movements I have encountered in just my own slight experience. People believe very little in spirit, yet it is precisely spirit that is needed to make this movement; what matters is its not being a one-sided result of a frigid, sterile necessity; the more it is that, the more doubtful it always is that the movement is proper.[2]

Of course others might take the view that the difficulty of the adjust-
ment was entirely proper given the horror of what his God had in-
flicted on Abraham. And, even were it not so, that literature is just
as concerned with getting things wrong as getting them right. Nonetheless it worried Kierkegaard that when something bad turns suddenly good again, he might not manage the change, the transition,
with simple grace or immediate happiness, but instead would be
thinking, doubting, or protesting behind-time in a grudging struggle
to re-adapt.

A pure or proper movement would consist in the graciousness
of a particular action, the intuitive clearing of doubt or the recognition of need, the finding of a right word or a good thought. All
of these are a success in life, the life of the spirit working instinctively, without that awkwardness of transition between thinking
and doing that so often occurs in the slow cranking movements
and ungainly compromises of common existence. As Kierkegaard
says elsewhere:

In the life of the spirit there is no standing still (everything is actuation);
therefore, if a person does not do what is right at the very second he knows
it—then, first of all, knowing simmers down, and willing allows some time
to elapse, an interim called: 'We shall look at it tomorrow.' During all this,
knowing becomes more and more obscure, and the lower nature gains the
upper hand more and more; alas, for the good must be done immediately,
as soon as it is known (and that is why in pure ideality the transition from
thinking to being is so easy, for there is everything at once), but the lower
nature's power lies in stretching things out.[3]

In the quick opening of the sheer moment of possibility, it does not
matter whether what is happening happens in doing or in thinking,
in writing or in reading, or whatever the realm. For which it is, in
the midst of concentration and the instant of occurrence, one may
hardly know or care. '*Everything* is actuation.' In the life of the spirit,
or the realm of ideality as Kierkegaard also calls it, you do whatever
it is fast, you know it in the very doing of it, and everything comes
'at once'—meaning both 'together' and 'immediately'—for there
are no divisions and no categories. This is the rare place at the ideal
moment where in the density of mental compression you may find
those half-lost first things—or as Johnson put it, 'systems in their ele-

ments, actions in their motives'. It would take ages to spell out every thought or motion that went into such a moment of sudden unity in action.

So it is that in a novel by my teacher Stanley Middleton, an ordinary uncertain man faces his unhappy wife on her return from an affair on an opera tour abroad. 'You will never be able to forget what I've done to you. It'll always be there in your mind,' she says to him, and again: 'You won't be able to forget what I've done, will you.' It is very plausible that an attempted reunion may be no more than the temporary papering of cracks, for a whole series of mixed motives on both sides. There are obvious doubts, disclaimers, and qualifications that rightly can and should be made—if any such couple could indeed logically go through them, one by one. 'But what you don't realize,' the husband suddenly replies, 'is how glad I am to see you sitting in this room, telling me you're going to stay.' This novel then says: 'As soon as he established it in words it became the truth.'[4] *He* didn't realize it either. It *became* the truth is like that famous return of E. M. Forster in *Aspects of the Novel*: 'How do I know what I think till I see what I say?' An uncertain man hears his own words giving him conviction on the rebound. It is not that language is inadequate, as the cliché has it: it can be a hundred times more adequate than most other things in this world. Through simple words, this is suddenly a pure movement found and made within a difficult, impure, human space: here a wife returned, there a son given back. In the rich interaction between active and passive, the creature suddenly makes himself creative.

But often it is more like this instead, from Bernard Malamud's *The Assistant* (1957). Frank Alpine knows that he ought to confess to his employer, the poor Jewish grocer, that he was one of the masked men who had held him up in his own store; that in fact he had become his assistant in disguised reparation for the crime. Frank can't get straight, he can't earn the love of the grocer's daughter, if this confession doesn't come first. From the minute he had committed the crime

he had got this sick feeling that he might some day have to vomit up in words, no matter how hard or disgusting it was to do, the thing he was then engaged in doing. He felt he had known this, in some frightful way, a long time before he went into the store...that he had really known all his life he would some time, through throat blistered with shame, his eyes in the dirt, have to tell some poor son of a bitch that he was the one who had hurt or betrayed him.

'Whatever had happened had happened wrong': he had to 'change the beginning, beginning with the past'—this is the syntax of the awkward position, the clumsy blocked movement struggling to disentangle itself from within its own midst. 'The impulse came on him to spill everything now, *now*'—even now, belatedly, to do what is right at the very second he knows it. But—

but it was like tearing up your whole life, with the broken roots and blood; and a fear burned in his gut that once he had got started saying the wrongs he had done he would never leave off...

He would have to say so much—himself, speaking in evidence against himself—that there would seem to be no self left to do all that confessing and survive it. Frank sees the primary necessity of the pure deed so clearly but in the dense mess of ordinary life he cannot carry it out, and that tormenting inability becomes for this recidivist as he repeats his errors and his sins a long-lasting and terrible holding-place. 'Purgatory,' says George Steiner, 'is the natural locus of the arts' even when it exists only on earth, here in a common grocer's shop. But that is not the place where the divine comedy ends.

What is *the place of literature?*

In Chapter 2, I offered two concluding ideas concerning literature's holding-ground, as it was conceived in Chapter 1. The first was near the end of section 1, where it was argued that literature, and poetry in particular, could become a place where whatever was humanly important could stay, as it were, communing with itself, speaking and hearing itself in one. The second at the end of section 2 argued that this place was nonetheless sited not so much *within* some autonomous realm of literature but in an arena immaterially existent somewhere *between* literature and life. It is only when he finished a painting, said Lucien Freud, that he was surprised and disappointed to find that it *was* only a painting after all. In the midst of it all, it had seemed more like—we might say—Kierkegaard's realm of ideality in which everything has the immediacy and reality of action. At the moment of the most intense formulation, at the moment of the most absorbed reading, it is not clear *where* one—a writer, a painter, a speaker, or a reader—really is at all. Nor does it matter: at least somewhere, somehow, in the world this thought is being realized, this deed done. Only on completion does the action become only itself again in all the imperfections of compromise and outcome: it was, after all, a painting or a poem that still fell short of being all that its artist had first intended it to be, had felt it was standing for in its still undetermined midst. That is why Ruskin loved Turner or, equivalently in literature, the apparent carelessness of a Byron: they made the lack of perfect finish part of the work's own language-within-language, limitation used as a sign of approximation to point to more than itself. Little intimations of the raw intent that went *into* the work, but could not find perfect expression there in its realization, are handed on to seek completion in the imagination of the person who reads the book or sees the painting.

That is the secret and almost impossible message sent by the more naive second or under-language in a work of literature: Understand me; find those first things that went into me within you. This is what I think Tolstoy really meant when he said in *What is Art?* that through speech humans communicate their thoughts and their intents but through art they communicate their feelings. Not that those feelings do not contain thoughts, but rather that they quickly contain how to 'take' those thoughts, offering beyond the literal the excess of what it is like to feel them. The message is finally conveyed immaterially.

In *The Singularity of Literature* (2004) Derek Attridge argued that literature is not predictable or solid enough 'to serve a political or moral programme', nor is it susceptible to an instrumental approach that seeks 'to comprehend the text by relating it to known and fixed parameters and values'. Literature 'solves no problems and saves no souls'. I agree with this refusal of the over-literal and over-programmatic. But it is hard to see from this account what literature *does* do. It is the 'elusive pleasures' of the literary, its ethical respect for the sheer 'otherness' of existence, that Attridge praises. But is not this a sophisticated return to the old aestheticism, art for art's sake, artefacts safely too complex for translation in any form? I do not want familiarized reductiveness or moralistic didacticism, as though literature were no more than a set of self-help books, but nor do I want wholly to rid myself of the purposive question too often dismissed as merely instrumentalist: what is this *for*? how can I properly *use* the literary? The crude and the raw, as original needs, are still part of the endeavour however much the endeavour rightly transforms and sophisticates them.

I readily grant that it is in many ways a strangely immaterial place that literature occupies in the world. It need not be purgatory, though it is a middle state. Look at a reader thinking of what he or she is reading. What you see, says Proust, are the 'distant' eyes of those who are manifestly thinking 'about something else'. Where is the thinking and imagining going on? It visibly seems to be going on behind the eyes, behind the forehead; yet *in* there the thinker will be thinking of somewhere else, some other time, some other thing. Proust would look up from his reading, 'my eyes still fixed on some point one would in vain have looked for in the room or outside'.[5]

But I want to claim finally that literature is something going on *within* that outside world, and not least through its readers. So far from being wholly 'other', it both necessarily involves and tacitly still calls for a strong relation to the non-literary and the extra-literary— even implicitly in its purest and most successful moments of sheer being. 'It is great to grasp hold of the eternal,' says Kierkegaard, 'but greater to hold fast to the temporal having given it up.' He says it of Abraham, but it is true too of literature itself: it keeps returning us from that higher level it creates, back into the life which is its subject matter. That said, what always comes *first* is the emotional belief in literature and in what is inside literature—before anyone can know where the meaning has come from, what to do with it, or where it can go.

1. Holding-ground, not framework

Paradigm crises

Many years ago a famous piece of work was done by T. S. Kuhn, in a book entitled *The Structure of Scientific Revolutions*, published in 1962.

Kuhn argued that rather than gradually developing in a continuous linear manner, the whole framework of human understanding changed suddenly and radically at critical moments in the history of thinking, through what he called major paradigm-shift. At such crisis-points a number of discordant facts would emerge that no longer easily fitted into the old way of seeing, until in reaching a critical mass, the data became so unbearably anomalous as no longer to make tenable the existent world-view. When those discrepancies were few or new, they were barely even recognized within the old order of understanding: an extraordinary comment on the way forms and frames determine or occlude content. But at some great tipping-point, the anomalies become too many, too consciously visible for the old order to hold. Within years of each other in the first decades of the seventeenth century, for example, Galileo and Kepler, following the earlier work of Copernicus, turned the belief that the sun revolves around the earth into a counter-realization that the earth revolves around the sun. The equivalent revolution in the nineteenth century took place when Paley's world-view, in which everything fitted so beautifully and perfectly into its place in the Creation through the wisdom of its Creator, gave way to Darwin's radical inversion, whereby everything was in its place only because of all else that had been forced out of it, in the crowded competitive struggle for life that went on within limited room and resources. So too with Kant's own so-called Copernican Revolution, or with Marx's inversion of Hegel: every system seems to have within it the kernel of its own destruction or replacement. Applicable beyond the realm of science, Kuhn's work made one ask, of any particular time, what kinds of thought were thinkable, what kinds were not.

There are what Kierkegaard might describe as great pure movements of decisive shift—Abraham's in faith, Galileo's in cosmology, Darwin's in biology. But what interests me every bit as much as that moment *after* the heuristic shift into the new order is the crisis moment just *before*, that was in need of it. That moment, however long it lasts, constitutes the barely articulable experience of a half-way reality, a reality imaginably in between frameworks, almost impossible to realize or locate.

There is a wonderful moment at the very end of Spenser's *The Faerie Queene* when the figure of Mutability says to the world that nothing lasts, nothing stays. To this Nature must then make reply, whilst knowing in her heart of hearts that it is true. It is not so much what she replies that I want to concentrate on here—though she replies not by denying or utterly changing that framework but re-interpreting it, saying that change works not only to take away but also to bring back. But it is the moment just a second before that which marks the great transition:

> So having ended, silence long ensued,
> Ne* Nature to and fro spake for a space   [*Nor]
> But with firm eyes affixt, the ground still viewed.
> Meanwhile, all creatures, looking in her face,
> Expecting th'end of this so doubtful case,
> Did hang in long suspense what would ensue,
> To whether side should fall the sovereign place:
> At length, she looking up with cheerful view,
> The silence brake, and gave her doom* in speeches few. [*judgement]

She takes in this external view-point of Mutability's and while she stares, apparently at the ground, is seeing what if anything she finds surviving still within herself, from which to make reply. What have you got to say? is the great question.

And that epistemological crisis can occur in quite ordinarily personal situations too: someone secure in the belief of being highly valued by employers and colleagues is suddenly made redundant; someone proposed for membership of a club whose members were all close friends has the application abruptly turned down without explanation; someone falls out of love and needs to know how he or she can possibly have been so wrong about the other person; or, more happily, a person has the surprise of being loved or successful long after one had seemed to give up hope.[6] This is the territory of the anomalous that literature so often occupies for us, particularly perhaps in the holding form of the realist novel. It marks out what it imaginably feels like when your sense of the world no longer fits with the framework of sub-conscious assumptions under which you had previously worked. Your world has changed; your story is interrupted; you cannot see how where you are *now* relates to where you were *before*. All you have left is your baffling personal experience as powerful raw data in search of form.

To know the dilemma *inside* the ordinary, to know it emotionally *within* the personal, to know it in the small and from the bottom: this is what can make this experience most real to most of us, and not just intellectually notional. But it makes the felt situation also in need of further help, stranded as it is in its new dilemma of lost trust or shocked disorientation. It is then that the personal sees how much *more* than the personal it needs: how much, for example, the personal now truly *needs* the philosopher to be created within itself to give counsel on the problem of other minds, or personal continuity, or ambiguous interpretation, or the relation of possible thoughts to the frameworks that allow them. And this requirement is prior to that terrible division of labour through formalized specialization that may separate the study of philosophy, or psychology, or theology, from the human situations that make them necessary. In this way the personal situation, invented or re-created within a literary work, is also always potentially a metaphor for—a way into the necessity of—what is *more* than personal, the big thoughts bursting out of the ostensibly small occasions that prompt them. This is what, say, George Eliot's *Middlemarch* exists in the world to establish. 'Not that this inward amazement of Dorothea's was anything very exceptional', says George Eliot of her young newly married protagonist caught in transition, the novelist seeking to bridge any all-too-easily assumed gap between novel and world: 'Nor can I suppose that when Mrs Casaubon is discovered in a fit of weeping six weeks after her wedding, the situation will be regarded as tragic.' Some discouragement when the new real future replaces the imaginary is, George Eliot concedes, 'not unusual, and we do not expect people to be deeply moved by what is not unusual'. Then this, without concession at all:

That element of tragedy which lies in the very fact of frequency, has not yet wrought itself into the coarse emotion of mankind; and perhaps our frames could hardly bear much of it. If we had a keen vision and feeling of all ordinary human life, it would be like hearing the grass grow and the squirrel's heart beat, and we should die of that roar which lies on the other side of silence. As it is the quickest of us walk about well wadded with stupidity. (*Middlemarch* (1871–2), chapter 20)

The realist novel in such hands is itself a sort of 'paradigm shift' that nonetheless retains the framework which it also challenges from within, tacitly saying: the framework of ostensible normality deceives us as to what is *really* going on within it. It is not that literature has no such blind spots, though in a writer's frequent relish for incongruities it probably has fewer: it is rather that, when full to the brim of challenging content, its own blind spots are more likely to be imagined, exposed, and even recognized. 'The quickest of us walk about well-wadded with stupidity.' But the novel itself is not stupid, is not merely descriptive or empirical, when it is saturated with too many thoughts about reality to make for one simple idea of it. We prefer to think one thing at a time, at most two things and then most conveniently in contrast; but three or four or five or more in a complex blending, and we don't even recognize that this is thinking. Try counting the thoughts in a powerful paragraph in a realist novel: they are no longer separate units. That apparently undefined richness then becomes the human thinking it truly is—literary thinking carried out in terms of human beings, within what they are and do. And the writers of literature seem to keep saying: anything can be thought and made into thought's subject matter, ahead of its being a recognized discipline, or having a compartmentalized category for itself.

The example of 'Shakespeare thinking'
But it is always Shakespeare—and what I will call 'Shakespeare thinking'—that is the epitome of the literary here, by offering human material which seems to be dynamically prior to *any* framework that tries to constrain it.

Think of the great and terrible inexhaustible moment in *King Lear* when the blinded Gloucester, made suicidal, stands on the heights of Dover; the anguished witness his banished and now disguised son, Edgar, leading him on, along the level ground of the stage, while the cliff is made safely non-existent save in the imagination of Gloucester's mind's eye:

GLOUCESTER: Methinks the ground is even.
EDGAR: Horrid steep.
Hark! Do you hear the sea?
GLOUCESTER: No, truly.

EDGAR: Why then your other senses grow imperfect
By your eyes' anguish.

Disguised as a poor peasant by means of false accent, Edgar does to blind Gloucester's aural universe what Shakespeare himself does anyway, use words to describe what is not there, deluding the blind father into what he hopes at worst will be a safe attempt at suicide. It is a moment of trial and test that a Kierkegaard or a Conrad would understand, in fear and trembling:

GLOUCESTER: Set me where you stand.
EDGAR: Give me your hand. You are now within a foot
Of th'extreme verge.

This is no ordinary framework. That 'foot' is literal though the 'verge' is not: the physical realm and Gloucester's mental version of it, the one materially visible, the other invisible, are *both* of them there on stage in wholly different dimensions of being, held simultaneously together. This dense and unpartitioned intervolvedness, the equivalent of the painter's cubism, is the great characteristic of the Shakespeare universe, causing sensations which are as paradoxically rebounding to the mind as the experience of seeing a blind man *not* able to see. Theatre—this most visual of media—here plays off the visible not only against the oral but against the invisible too. It is as though the scene has more senses intermixed in it than it has protagonists, and has become a complex living thing in itself.

'Let go my hand,' says Gloucester, making the peasant leave him, 'and let me hear thee going.' We see two men on stage but know that there are also three, the son as peasant counting twice. And we almost see Gloucester's deceived imagination in the very postures of his swaying body. Then Edgar makes the noise of tramping feet, and in that psychic separating the peasant does begin to leave and stand apart, while the son himself stays still within inches of the old man:

EDGAR [*ASIDE*]:   Why I do trifle thus with his despair
Is done to cure it.
GLOUCESTER: O you mighty gods.
[*He kneels*]
This world I do renounce, and in your sights
Shake patiently my great affliction off.
If I could bear it longer, and not fall

> To quarrel with your great opposeless wills,
> My snuff and loathed part of nature should
> Burn itself out. If Edgar live, O bless him!
> Now fellow, fare thee well.
> EDGAR: Gone, sir, farewell

And then Gloucester falls forward, not hundreds of feet downward, but a few inches flat onto his face.

Challenged by all that goes on here, there is one major point I want to emphasize, though it may seem very small. But it is like Shakespeare that the secrets of his making should be placed off-centre and as though incidentally, in the act of the making itself. Thus: actually, neither in quarto nor in folio is there the explicit stage-direction 'aside' when Edgar speaks out loud. Like a live audience, like imaginative actors themselves, readers of the original texts have rather to realize that it is 'aside' in the full unguided strangeness of happening: all the dimensions of reality are there—you have to work out what is happening where and why without signalling; you have to reassemble the different planes and modalities of life immediately in front of you. It is just a quick micro-change of expected word—Edgar says '*his* despair' not 'your despair'—and at the macro-level everything changes with that, as in an earthquake's tremor from below upwards. It is like Shakespeare's sparing use of punctuation as far as it can be gauged from a manuscript fragment of *Sir Thomas More*: he didn't want much, he mainly left it to the lineation; he wanted one thing to pass into another, almost before one knew it. *Then*, perhaps a micro-second later, you registered the anomalies, the significant variations, making changes in realization from a level just below ordinary consciousness. We as readers and as audience have to *make* sense of it as we go, as if the drama were indeed a form of living action rather than clod-hopping summary or framed caricature.

This is 'Shakespeare thinking'. He transforms the static convention of the crude, behind-the-hand explanatory aside to the audience into what Kierkegaard might call a distinct if still awkward 'movement' in the world. In Edgar 'Why I do trifle thus' exists uncomfortably side-by-side with the process it cannot now interfere with on this stage, at once so near to *and* far from the father. It cannot be a silent thing, as Cordelia once was: it must have all the helpless clumsiness of exposed and risky intention painfully blurted out into the world, by the terrible reality of which it will finally be tested. It is like a very serious adult version of Charles Fernyhough's child, speaking thought out loud in the world. For Shakespeare's is a world in which thinking happens out there, collaboratively even in the conflicts, between people even when it is also within them; a world which, even as we *see* its internal separatenesses, is heard as one acoustic whole, full of different sounds and noises.

What happens in Shakespeare thinking is not at all like paraphrase of solid character and straightforward story—Gloucester tries to commit suicide while his son watches him—but is more like existential physics. That is to say, the very universe seems dramatically to morph. Ground rises up into cliff and falls back down to ground again. One man stands within inches of another and yet that other cannot hear him, as though suddenly they were in split-screen separate but parallel universes whilst still also on the same world-stage. The law in 'Shakespeare thinking' is that thoughts and the persons to which they relate belong right up against each other, on stage at the same time, no matter their different ontologies. Shakespeare loved to appear crowdingly indiscriminate, packing his lines with mixed realities. It was how the life-principle itself seemed to Shakespeare to work from the very beginning—agnostically ignoring potential distinctions until or unless they had to make themselves come into distinct being and happen in the world. He was daring to replicate or transcribe the processes of that life-principle, first on page and then on stage—as if this was life happening for the first time again, where all the elements of being were crowded together for anything to emerge in this model of a world. Characters are forces in an energy-field, more like parts of verbs than nouns. Coriolanus, for instance, is not simply a set character: within his visible human shape he is more truly a god of war, a sword of the republic, the embodiment of Rome itself waiting for his elemental force to be activated, his identity merged into action in the world. Only in the aftermath or from outside is he by default an ego again.

There is not just 'communication' in all this, there are electric flashes of contact and re-formation across the Shakespearean stage.

When Gloucester blindly cries 'If Edgar live, O bless him! | Now
fellow, fare thee well': the 'fellow' on that instant has been re-made
into 'Edgar' alongside him, suddenly feeling himself 'Edgar' as from
within his own father's mind. At such moments in the crossing of
ostensibly solid physical boundaries, reality is something that *happens*.
The whole Shakespearean world suddenly twists and morphs in response to such change within itself. And in such a world, no experiment or venture can remain predictably under control. Edgar now
rushes to his fallen father's side, thinking: This was meant to be safe;
physically it was only a few feet to fall face-forward:

> Now fellow, fare thee well.
> EDGAR: Gone, sir, farewell
> *Gloucester falls*
> [*Aside*] And yet I know not how conceit may rob
> The treasury of life, when life itself
> Yields to the theft. Had he been where he thought
> By this had thought been past.—Alive or dead?
> Ho you, sir! Hear you, sir? Speak.
> [*Aside*] Thus might he pass indeed. Yet he revives
> What are you, sir?
> GLOUCESTER: Away and let me die

The changes marked as asides are no more than the simplest index
of the shifts in reality's framework that are going on here, and once
again the signalling of them is in neither quarto nor folio but is a
slowed-down modern editorial interpellation. Here is another set of
voices, another disguise, when the man at the foot of the supposed
cliff is not the same as the peasant at the top of it. But more deeply
telling is the way that the very reality now turns from the physical
outside into the psychological within, as though what was seen on
stage was geared to the very twist of the suicidal syntax: 'had he
been where he *thought* | By this had *thought* been past'. For this
moment, 'where he thought' is where the play's focus now is: inside
the head of an unconscious man, where the mere imagination ('con-
ceit') that he has fallen may have had sufficient reality, after all, to
have killed him.

But Gloucester's reviving 'Away and let me die' is then coun-
tered by Edgar saying, 'Thy life's a miracle': for at those four
words the world tilts again, the revealed meaning being *more* than

the literal and physical sense, though acted out within it. A life is a miracle. 'Have I fallen or no?' asks Gloucester in this see-saw of reality. 'Do but look up,' his companion urges, in reply. And then in another twist Gloucester must reply: 'Alack, I have no eyes.' There, suddenly, it feels as though Gloucester were blinded all over again, in a rapid reconfiguration of time, now, as much as space.

It is not characters, it is not stories, it is not themes or images or ideologies that are the hallmark of Shakespeare thinking. Western philosophy is mainly a philosophy of things, of names and substances. Its idea of knowledge seeks the consolidating status of permanence. It needs to corral the accidents of contingent time, in their evasion of higher category or single cause, into a framework of meaning. But Shakespeare said of existence, and of the thinking that must go on within and not merely above it, what Galileo said of the earth: it *moves*. It is more like verb than noun. 'Make thick my blood,' cries Lady Macbeth, 'Stop up th'access and passage to remorse' (*Macbeth*, 1.5.42–3): remorse is not simply a concept or a thing, it is a potential motion in and through the very bloodstream. It is even that tiny micro-word 'to', more than 'of', that makes it so dangerously invasive. Likewise, Macbeth is not simply 'a guilty man': he can feel his secret Guilt breaking out from within him as if it were in its own right now an invisible reality—'Come, let me clutch thee | I have thee not, and yet I see thee still' (2.1.34–5)—the dagger of the guilty act visible to him alone as guilt itself threatens to become a bigger reality than he has.

This swift Shakespearean mobility across ontological dimensions may be best conveyed to modern minds by what William James, John Dewey, and A. N. Whitehead were doing at the beginning of the twentieth century with Process Philosophy. For them, existence consists in events before things, verbs ahead of nouns, change and flow and process rather than stasis and fixity. The primary realities are momentary happenings, not separate objects or pre-established forms. The grammar of life is not subject-verb-object chopped up and then ploddingly linked together by a steady serial logic. Events and occasions are created when elements of the universe come together to make something out of themselves regardless of separate consciousnesses. In the classical mathematical physics that Newton

118 *Reading and the Reader*

was to bring to Shakespeare's world, space and time were made external to the entities that make up the universe: they served as the fundamental receptacle or frame of reference into which the content of the world was inserted. But in Shakespeare each happening dramatically changes the shape and frame of its world in a moment— or as Process philosophers were to put it, each occasion re-creates space-time in and around itself, as part of its very occurrence.

Shakespeare's words are not just slotted into a pre-formed grammar-box; his protagonists are not just defined by a set name or concept; and his thoughts and his people are not merely contained within the bounds of a settled world. That would be second-order work where Shakespeare's is quintessentially primary. In this chapter I am talking about imprisonment within frameworks, breaking out of frameworks, being in transition between frameworks; but here with Shakespeare you see the neutral striving thing itself—the variety of human existence within the ground-plan of the world—working its way through some primary living process larger than any frame or form it must only temporarily inhabit. Copernicus and Kepler assembled so many anomalies as made them change the current framework of astronomical understanding even from within it. But in Shakespeare, in literary thinking at its most linguistically unfettered, *every* point of thought is not so much an anomaly as itself potentially—to use Keats's phrase in a letter of 13 March 1818— 'the centre of an intellectual world'. No category of thought can hold all those potential worlds. Shakespeare and the seeds in his work can out-grow and break up any framework.

The venture for meaning

There was a mantra that the Nigerian writer Wole Soyinka repeated in extremis throughout the time of his imprisonment, in the dark of solitary confinement—the artistic saying of Picasso, '*I do not seek, I find.*' A man of words, he was reliant on these words. But he kept hold of them not now for the artistic purposes that had got him into trouble with the government in the first place, but for their use within purposes of survival. For Soyinka, struggling in his cell against the formless psychic assaults on his identity, that saying was a touchstone. It kept recalling a sort of small inner instinct of being at his core, resiliently waiting to be triggered.

Picasso's statement replaced in this prisoner what would have seemed to Soyinka too large, too assertively unsupported to stand the test of extremity: namely, 'the *conscious* quest for the inner self'. Distrustful of his own normal consciousness as though it were a falsifying framework in which a false messenger was all too inclined to dramatize itself, Soyinka used 'I do not seek, I find' to say: 'Let actions alone be the manifestation of the authentic being in defence of its authentic visions.'[7]

I have been arguing that such actions can happen anywhere—not just in deeds, but in opportunities for mind, in solitary, on page, in speech, in reading. We are probably, perhaps inevitably, trapped in false frameworks, in a disabling world-view. But no system can be right in which experience cannot exceed the extent to which it is known. Consciousness cannot take the lead but needs to be informed by something other than and prior to itself, that waits 'to find' its prompt and its chance within an agnostic holding-ground of experience.

My claim is not that it is either possible or desirable wholly to avoid frameworks, if we are indeed to follow Bion's warning on how vital it is to find an apparatus of thinking by which to have our thoughts. Nor is it that thoughts and feelings can arise purely and innocently from below, as if they were not already influenced by implicit frameworks acquired as second nature throughout the course of a life. But in literary thinking three factors characteristically take us beyond the over-literal application of pre-established programming. One is the saturating multiplicity of overlapping factors involved in the re-creation of any significant human situation; second is the power, range, and historical depth of the language at its free maximum, yielding to thought something more than a contemporary exercise in labelling; third is the presence of a second person, a second pair of eyes, created by the opportunity to reflect upon and test out equivalent selves in situations analogous to one's own, with more time in which to hold such contemplation than any first person ever has in the immediate thick of things.

So it is that literature is vital within the modern problems of finding meaning. Alasdair MacIntyre's great provocative book *After Virtue* (1981) offers the thesis of a modern world incoherently made up only of the broken fragments of many different disciplines, traditions, frameworks, and languages from the past, the rival claims of which are now unsettlable. Imagine a Catastrophe in the world of Science, he says at the beginning of his book, in which a whole body of knowledge is suddenly destroyed by a tribe of barbarians. When in the aftermath the survivors try to piece together what is left, all they have are fragments, the results of experiments detached from the theoretical contexts that gave them meaning, instruments whose use has been forgotten. But the greater disaster in this scenario is that nobody quite realizes that they no longer know what they are doing. That is, says MacIntyre, an analogy for what he thinks of as an *unrecognized* catastrophe in the world of morality, meaning, and purpose inherited in our times. It is like an incoherent Babel of wildly different voices, from many different times and sources, heard in the head.

But I am arguing that the rich repository of that diaspora and that confusion is literature and the agnostic or aesthetic realm it holds open. And that makes it a site for venture and not just of catastrophe.

2. Translation

'The poetic experience' and 'lifting our eyes from the page'
In an essay on 'Embodiment and Incarnation' in poetry, Les Murray remembers a conversation he had about a particular poem, not his own, with a serious but everyday reader whom he knew well:

'I came to that place in the poem,' as a friend said to me once, 'and clunk! my mind turned inside out, quite painlessly. "Huh?" I said, and read that bit again, and it happened again, precisely there, and I couldn't explain it to myself.'[8]

That is what the poem is here—the reader's mind turned inside out. The thinking going on, on that page, seems to belong not just to words but to a mind lodged there; a mind, moreover, now seemingly thinking its thoughts in the reader, and the reader's in it, the distinction between the two at its most interesting when no longer clear. It is a great experiment to find whether that key place in the poem is still there, feeling the same, the next time Murray's friend returns to it. For that indeed is what he does find: there that centre is again, momentary and yet repeatable even in its surprise. In teaching, in reading-groups, that deictic function—no meta-talk, no explanation, just that initial wordless ability to locate and point to the poetic place—is the crucial first alternative to paraphrase from within conventional frameworks, to conceptual take-over bids, or to the summary expression of pieties.

Of this 'poetic experience'—of returning to the same charged space, be it in prose or verse, and finding it still hold good, like an island within the world—Murray concludes with this warning: 'We can have it repeatedly, and each time timelessly, but we can't have it steadily. We are as it were not yet permitted to live there.' We need the extra emotional lift-off to remind us of what human life can be. 'A bolt is shot back somewhere in our breast.' We need literature at least to help keep us longer in a place, a mood, or a mentality that we cannot long inhabit on our own. This means we need literature to hold for us even what we cannot fully retain or live up to.

And equally in turn, a reader cannot simply stay with the books or remain inside them. For one thing, the reader needs to stop reading in order to think hard and read well again. And this not merely lest bookishness become all-consuming. I mean rather that readers rightly often find themselves *not* reading, as such, in the midst of a book, but suddenly thinking instead. Or they walk away from a book only to find themselves still thinking about some small part of it in their own terms. Something of it stays with them to return years later in a new context of life. It is very important not always to respect and remain within the book's whole form. Otherwise the reader can be locked into the artifice, or the depersonalized institution, or the introverted habit, as if a book were a thing on its own, set in stone, a seamless timeless de-humanized classic. The book is not just there, where it appears to be.

The French poet Yves Bonnefoy has a fine essay translated as 'Lifting our Eyes from the Page', in which he has a word to say against over-professionalized reading that stays wholly within the text.[9] The writers themselves did not do that in the writing of it, says Bonnefoy, that is not how the so-called texts were themselves created:

Readers who write only by extracting from the pages of another and accumulating (for the sake of their own interpretations) simple elements of meaning, or aspects of their stylistic dimension, are thereby condemned to a use of words whose pre-eminently conceptual character—that is to say, abstract and without direct knowledge of the things that are exposed to time and finitude—can only deaden what in Rimbaud's or Artaud's works, or in so many others, was joy or suffering experienced more directly, more violently.... One might fear that it is reduced to nothing so much as a game—a game without any other responsibility than intellectual—whereas the work studied might, on the other hand, have been an experience in the tragedy of life.

Where it came from (in a Rimbaud or an Artaud, in a Dickens or a Conrad) is still somewhere imaginably contained within what it now is: the work has an aura around it, traces of what made it come into being, still left within that being. The ostensibly completed text has to free itself, says Bonnefoy, even from its own network of significations, even from its own carefully worked form, to be made alive in a reader in his or her own way. That is not in the least to say that its language does not matter, but rather that its language must morph into its meaning. Of course the unavoidable risk is that the bequeathed meaning which a reader takes away may as easily become lost or distorted as enriched in its new personal embodiment. Re-reading is important in checking and refreshing that sense of meaning, as the reader goes back and re-enters the precise language once again, as Murray's friend did. But the work is portable, must be transportable, as though itself needing to be restored to some thinking-place, some person, *outside* the text that is analogous to where and who it came from in the first instance. Otherwise, unless readers act as their users and their agents, the books stay inside themselves, in Plato's cave of institutionalized unreality.

Interruption, says Bonnefoy, is vital: walking away from a book in order to come back to it at a different level or in a new context; being able to leave oneself in order to look at oneself; unexpectedly allowing in some thought or memory that is more riskily informal, more unevenly related, than what might follow for the one-track mind. These are the to-and-fro ways of literary thinking. For interruption goes on within the poetry itself rather than its being seamless: the half-written, the unfinished, the jaggedly unruly should have their intrusive place within the written and the literary, says Bonnefoy, disrupting the tendency of literature to become a world of its own. Think of the interrupting space, for example, between the end of the first and the beginning of the second stanza in George Herbert's great poem 'The Flower', on recovery from depression:

> Grief melts away
> Like snow in May,
> As if there were no such cold thing.
>
> Who would have thought my shrivel'd heart
> Could have recover'd greenness? It was gone
> Quite under ground...

The total disappearance of what had previously seemed so absolutely insuperable is sudden and astounding: the poet doesn't 'move on', he needs rather to go back for a second thought, another attempt from a different angle, to try to find the underlying continuity, the story or explanation of his sudden shift from a human winter to a human spring. Or be amazed at explanation's absence. Who would have thought, indeed, of that beginning to the poem's second stanza? It would not be there, as a thing in the world, had Herbert not thought of saying it. No one would ask for it; no one would know if it had not been written, or would miss it. The poem exists in mid-air, so to speak, with no prior justification save its own existence as representative of what otherwise would have no place, or be merely elusive, in the world.

'The text is not poetry's true place,' Bonnefoy concludes in a crucial sentence, 'It is only the path it followed.'

Literature's shifting place

But what and where, then, is 'the true place' of literature in the world and for the future? Some of the speculative thinking that has been done about reading over the last few years suggests that there are good reasons why that true place is not easy to locate or appreciate. It may be useful to summarize three fundamental suggestions before making some final effort at conclusion.

First, reading and writing are not natural or immediate processes—as every struggling child-learner well knows. Neuroscientists now argue that reading is the result of exaptation, where an ancient biological function—in this case, the evolved cortical capacity for the visual identification of objects—is adapted to serve a purpose different from that for which it originally evolved. At the primitive level, the hunters did 'read' the material world, but did so naturally: 'They decipher animal tracks with amazing ease. Meticulous inspection of broken branches or faint tracks in the dirt allows them to quickly figure out what animal has been around, its size, the direction in which it went, and a number of other details that will be invaluable for hunting.'[10] Within this evolved cortical specialization for following the visible traces of animal tracks is lodged the later development of a more artificial reading-system for the de-coding of meaning. No wonder then that we best learn words, not through vocabulary lists, but through the very effort to hunt—to go *after* and get through to—the meaning of things, albeit modified by a later and necessarily acquired patience in understanding.

Secondly, the evolved writing and reading system is itself on the very borderline between the material and the immaterial. In Egyptian hieroglyphic writing, the sign for house looks like a house, albeit seen from above as the gods might: it is a material replication of a material object. But the development of a phonetic alphabet meant that the word looks nothing like the thing it stands for. The mind must now make the de-coding not from a simply transcribed version of direct perception but by using much more innerly complex mental processes of translation.[11]

This is further emphasized by the great shift from an oral to a written culture, where language-as-spoken is direct, present, and transient within the stream of physical life, but language-as-written is something that can be looked at and examined, at some distance from the immediacy of the material world. In seeking to work between these two modes, literature serves to retain something of the life of the spoken within the mind of the written. What was spread out in the world becomes compressed within the mind, one written word bespeaking, say, ten unspoken ones and triggering their underlying presence in the mind.

These three shifts—from first-hand to second, from material to immaterial, from oral to written—speak of literature as something with the very status of metaphor, in its effort still to work itself between two worlds and prevent their separation. And if there is that adaptation to shift involved in the creation of literature, there is a corresponding translation involved in its reception. The reader, in imaginative response, can almost 'hear' the written words, 'hunt' for clues, 'see' the meaning in some variable sense of that verb, and feel as if a primary experience is being imagined or recalled, as a result of reading and writing being lodged within more direct brain-functions not originally designed for them. A reader is thus a trans-lator—and a translator not just *of* the signs but *between* the signs and what they refer to in the world of human experience. And maybe one step further, even at the risk of over-toppling: the reader is the one who seeks ways through which to try to embed literary thinking within the ethos and practice of the world itself.

Some personal readings

Such intense reading is not a pure, abstract, tidy, or tame business. George Steiner, somewhat reluctantly distinguishing 'the reader' from 'the critic', once said that for the reader what is involved in reading is something less professional and more personal: that with-out ever wanting to admit it publicly, the reader is the one that goes to a book always secretly hopeful that this time *this* work might be *the* work, offering revelation.[12] He or she knows well enough, of course, that it is naive to think so; but such is the primal ancient drive for the reader as an incorrigible hunter for meaning that the desire for the message abides, even though no literal answer could possibly suffice and the chastening of the appetite for over-directness is often necessary. Yet if on any particular occasion *this* book is, once again, not *the* book—knowing indeed there may never again be any such thing as *the* book, as the Bible once was—then something *in* this book, some one sentence perhaps, may be the smaller equivalent.

When John Bunyan read Luther's Commentary on Paul's Epistle to the Galatians, it wasn't otherness that he found: 'I found my condition in his experience, so largely and profoundly handled, as if his Book had been written out of my heart; this made me marvel' (*Grace Abounding to the Chief of Sinners*, 1666). When Bernard Mala-mud's recidivist Frank Alpine reads Dostoevsky, 'he felt a strange falling away from the printed page and had this crazy sensation he was reading about himself.' A girl had recommended the book to Frank: 'It's a novel,' she explained. 'I'd rather read the truth,' he said. 'It is the truth,' she had replied.

I have witnessed the faces of those I have read to: the sudden
barely restrained crumpling of the apparently robust young man,
hearing T. S. Eliot's 'Wait without hope | For hope would be hope
for the wrong thing'; the sad comic happiness of an aged woman
taking Andrew Aguecheek's part, '*I* was adored once'; the prisoners
or addicts hearing the ghost of Jacob Marley, 'I wear the chain I
forged in life. I made it link by link, and yard by yard...' Or this
from Frances Hodgson Burnett's *The Secret Garden*, read in a facility
for the elderly living on in difficulty:

One of the strange things about living in the world, is that it is only now
and then, one is quite sure one is going to live forever, and ever, and
ever. One knows it sometimes when one gets up at the tender solemn
dawn time, and goes out and stands alone, and throws one's head far
back, and looks up and up, and watches the pale sky slowly changing,
and flushing, and marvellous unknown things happening, until the east
almost makes one cry out, and one's heart stands still, at the strange
unchanging majesty of the rising of the sun, which has been happening
every morning, for thousands and thousands and thousands of years.
One knows it then for a moment or so, and one knows it sometimes
when one stands by oneself in a wood at sunset, and the mysterious deep
gold stillness, slanting through and under the branches, seems to be
saying slowly, again and again, something one cannot quite hear, however much one tries. Then sometimes the immense quiet of the dark blue
at night, with millions of stars waiting and watching, makes one sure; and
sometimes a sound of far-off music makes it true; and sometimes a look
in someone's eyes.

Only now and then, forever. In the transcription of the session,
Elaine, who has to live full-time in the care-home, can be seen
saying to her reader: 'That's a way of putting it, isn't it, Katie.... I
used to look at the stars when I was a child, from the front bedroom.
I could look at them forever. Gazing out of the window for hours
now... I love the stars. Must think I'm mad [laughs]. But I think of
one of them—That's *my* star—every time I see it.' The temporary
transcendence in making such things as stars or poems in some
sense your own; the risk and trust of saying 'mad' in such an institution; the staring out of the window in childhood or here where a
carer might otherwise think the person merely vacant: these are
vulnerable, valuable matters.

It cannot be right if these essential immediacies are there only for the first-time readers, or untutored people in extremis, and no longer remain essential to the teachers, or the professionals in media and academe.

The most full-scale imagination of what it might be like to read the story of your own life is the case of Scrooge in Dickens's *A Christmas Carol*, a work too often dismissed as if it were a simple, cosy, sentimentally festive thing. Actually, at some level, it is Dickens's version of art as revenge from below, both socially and psychologically: the crude and the raw in feeling let loose upon the affluently and cynically uncaring by the unassailable sophistication of the writing that presents it.

By a series of sophisticated time-shifts, the ghostly Spirits of Christmas Past, Present, and Future that visit Scrooge act as formidable and demanding counsellors on the very boundary between psychological and religious orderings. The Spirits require Scrooge painfully to read as it were the real book of his life, and in particular to see his memory as a thing no longer hidden away within himself distorting his character, but actually made into an external object in front of his eyes.

He is shown a schoolboy who was left behind on his own at school at Christmas time: his younger self.

'The school is not quite deserted,' said the Ghost. 'A solitary child neglected by his friends, is left there still.'
Scrooge said he knew it. And he sobbed.

No wonder the deserted boy he once was grew into the man who hated Christmas. Yet when the man thus sees the boy again, he cries for him as though indeed at some level the child was 'still' left there. Somewhere too the man still loves the compensatory human company of the books which the boy in his loneliness is intently reading, for suddenly old Scrooge throws himself back into the spirit of *Robinson Crusoe*, the book in the boy's hand, giving childish whoops of delight out loud:

Then, with a rapidity of transition very foreign to his usual character, he said, in pity for his former self, 'Poor boy!' and cried again....
'What is the matter?' asked the Spirit.
'Nothing,' said Scrooge. 'Nothing...'

It is not nothing. Pity for that former self is not the same as self-pity. Or, crucially, it is the same thing—only in a different place now. For almost immediately in another quick transition 'foreign to his usual character', Scrooge thinks of an equivalent boy singing a Christmas carol outside his house the previous night, whom he had unkindly turned away. Transitions are crucial. At such moments of psychological reorientation, it is as though hardened damage could be turned back into tender vulnerability, or memory turned round into imagination, without their being new faculties or new events, but rather in a new positioning instead.

And then there is Scrooge's old amiable employer Fezziwig, so different from the mean employer Scrooge has become, throwing a simple hearty Christmas party for his people. 'A small matter,' says the Spirit provokingly, 'to make these silly folk so full of gratitude.' All it cost Fezziwig was a mere three or four pounds—'Is that so much that he deserves this praise?'

'It isn't that,' said Scrooge, heated by the remark, and speaking unconsciously like his former, not his latter, self. 'It isn't that, Spirit. He has the power to render us happy or unhappy; to make our service light or burdensome; a pleasure or a toil. Say that his power lies in words and looks; in things so slight and insignificant that is impossible to add and count 'em up: what then? The happiness he gives, is quite as great as if it cost a fortune.' He felt the Spirit's glance, and stopped...

This is Scrooge first of all forgetting himself, in the best sense—in a natural warm passion of indignation that functions in memory of an underlying belief we thought he had lost or never even had. 'It isn't that, it isn't that, Spirit,' says his voice, audibly different from previous negatives. But then, in one of those awkward moral movements Kierkegaard describes, Scrooge remembers himself again, under the silent eye of his counsellor-Spirit, knowing what in contrast he himself has become. 'What is the matter?' asks the Ghost. 'Nothing,' replies Scrooge again; 'Something,' insists the Ghost. 'I should like to be able to say a word or two to my clerk just now,' Scrooge confesses, 'That's all.' 'Nothing', 'something', 'all': these are the signs of the struggle to turn himself round. That almost neurological interplay between 'foreign to his usual character', 'pity for his former self', and 'speaking unconsciously like his former, not his latter, self' is like being involved in a constant mental reconfiguration, such indeed as William James described as conversion. Still, in these difficult transitions between times and selves and frameworks, it is very hard seamlessly to translate those 'things so slight and insignificant that it is impossible to add them up' back into the larger norms and habits of one's being.

Yet that is the sort of translation a reader has to make in the most serious of encounters with what is read: to turn those small micromessages into large macro thoughts and effects, as the immediate explosive force of emotion already seems to be asking of us. Only, of course, we do not have guiding spirits and ghosts. For the most part we do indeed have or have had family backgrounds, parents, the early stages of education moral, religious, or psychological. But in the next and later stages of a life many people have lost or discarded counsellors or teachers or elders, early tenets or indoctrinations. There remain general frameworks, habitual routines, social conventions, more or less helpful or constraining. But ostensibly grown-up people are mainly left free and alone, in private, to continue going a little wrong or getting a little lost—and perhaps more than a little—with hardly anyone to notice or help. Then it is and there it is that books meet unspoken needs. Not to cure, not even perhaps directly to help, but at least to help think.

And this is nothing so simple as seeking self-identification with the characters in a novel or using books for direct relevance to one's own situation: that is not my argument, especially when I query whether the repertoires of consciousness or the idea of the self are actually the best frameworks within which to try to function. 'I do not seek, I find': readers rightly do not always know how or why what so personally 'finds' them in a book relates to them; only that somehow it must, for the connection and the recognition to have been forged. The literary work, being more than an over-specific manual, replaces the therapist or teacher, the set interpreter or group motivator, allowing the reader the emotional and imaginative freedom to become his or her own therapist, own philosopher, own experimental actor and imaginer, own adventuring individual, without having to join a party or a sect of ready-made messages and collective prescriptions.

Within the primary language of a work there is, I argued in Chapter 1, always literature's potential for a second or under-language—

the shorthand of condensed inner speech offered to a reader through a word or a phrase; an electric association of feeling or a pang of memory. These are the portables which, as Bonnefoy argues, are taken out of a text and into a life. 'And what I *feel*, across the inferior features | Of what I *am*', 'Strength came where weakness was not known to be', 'And now in age I bud again'.

Each reader has, as Iris Murdoch says, a collection of those special things, which become nascent sites for thinking and re-centring. These memorable fragments serve as metaphors for what readers, finding in these utterances a special voice for themselves, may or may not quite recall. Sometimes one knows well enough again what person or feeling or idea they are metaphors for; but the site or the metaphor always comes first, as the ground of meaning. This idea that the text contains within it a niche for its secret personal meaning to the reader, thinking off the back of the text, also is itself one of the secrets of reading.

There remains, then, the challenge that the naive and needy reader dares to represent—and which a great novelist is not ashamed to embed within one of her own novels. George Eliot refuses to seal literature off within itself, insists on the need to keep breaking down its frameworks even from within them. I am thinking again here of the earnest young woman, Maggie Tulliver, expressing within *The Mill on the Floss* the very desire for realism that the novel itself aspires to:

Sometimes Maggie thought she could have been contented with absorbing fancies; if she could have had all Scott's novels and all Byron's poems!— then, perhaps, she might have found happiness enough to dull her sensibility to her actual daily life. And yet they were hardly what she wanted. She could make dream-worlds of her own, but no dream-world would satisfy her now. She wanted some explanation of this hard, real life: the unhappy-looking father seated at the dull breakfast-table; the childish, bewildered mother; the little sordid tasks that filled the hours, or the more oppressive emptiness of weary, joyless leisure; the need of some tender, demonstrative love; the cruel sense that Tom didn't mind what she thought or felt, and that they were no longer playfellows together; the privation of all pleasant things that had come to *her* more than to others: she wanted some key that would enable her to understand, and in understanding, to endure, the heavy weight that had fallen on her young heart. (Book 4, chapter 3)

The father, the mother, Tom the brother: there is no syntax here, just a long list of unhappy bits and pieces. What Maggie wants is some key or what elsewhere in happier days she had also called link— 'something that would link together the wonderful impressions of this mysterious life, and give her soul a sense of home in it' (Book 3, chapter 5). And that means not only a link between the different parts of her world but also a link between what she read and how she lived. As the literary critic Michael Wood puts it, many works aspire to the condition of parables, seeming to ask of us 'not so much immediate action as a scene of application, a place in our lives where their analogies can come home as a form of the literal'—the literary seeking finally to re-inform the literal rather than merely eschew it.[13]

To meet that challenge of connection, in what follows I shall be relying a little more on books that lie on the boundary between life and literature, between factual and imaginative writing.

John Berger's case history

As a youth he had especially relished reading the work of Joseph Conrad because Conrad's stories of the sea created for him the ancient sense of some great natural test awaiting human beings in their passage through the world. Otherwise the youth could see nothing in the world immediately around him but tame convention and trivial monotony.

'Keep facing it,' said the usually uncommunicative MacWhirr to his young lieutenant at the height of the storm. Will the ship live through it? asks Jukes in return, as though inadvertently praying:

It was as unintentional as the birth of a thought in the head, and he heard nothing of it himself. It all became extinct at once—thought, intention, effort—and of his cry the inaudible vibration added to the tempest waves of the air.

He expected nothing from it. Nothing at all. For indeed what answer could he make? But after a while he heard with amazement the frail and resisting voice in his ear, the dwarf sound, unconquered in the giant tumult.
'She may!'[14]

'She may come out of it yet,' the captain repeats, in taciturn defiance of fearful imagination and natural chaos alike. MacWhirr's barely heard, hardly articulate words matter more than the mean-

ingless noise that almost engulfs them—they are like a real-life image
of what literature, the few crucially meant words, might do in the
world for those who need to hear them.

The youth, whose name was John Sassall, wanted that drama of
rescue-work in real life. In response to an emergency one was no
longer just a self, but rather an action tested out in the world, decisively involved in its changing. *You* went into *It*, the crisis, and *It*
then showed what there was in *You*. In that meeting and blending,
You tried to use yourself as an element within *It* to adjust or with-
stand *Its* force. That is why he decided to become a doctor: as
MacWhirr to the sea, so Sassall wished to be in relation to the crises
of sickness and accident, 'She may come out of it yet.' The doctor
calmly arrived on the scene, did something expert physically to heal
or save a life, and then moved on to the next emergency call.

Only of course it became more complicated for Sassall, when he
did actually become a doctor. As a day-to-day general practitioner
in a small country community, he had to take into account the less
dramatic, less easily treatable crises of his patients over years of
living amidst them. Gradually his vocation became less material and
less decisive, and more humanly imaginative. He became not so
much the fictional hero enjoying danger, the specialist arriving to
operate at the centre of a specific one-off physical crisis, but a figure
more on the circumference, a recorder and listener trying to understand his patients' difficulties in the context of their whole lives over
many years. Increasingly, illness was becoming for Sassall less like a
practical emergency, and more like an inarticulate language, a baffled, suffering form of expression that he had to read, interpret, and
respond to. It wasn't that he simply dismissed and outgrew all he
had got from Conrad in terms of the desire for mastery, skill, and
command in the face of untamed nature. He had also read excitedly
of Prometheus, Faust, and Paracelsus, figures who had dared to
want the knowledge of a god. In them he had found another ancient
idea: that of the universal man, the Renaissance man, capable of
working across all things, translating and combining all skills, mental
and physical, theoretical and practical, active and contemplative, in
one person. There was of course a good portion of personal egotism,
of raw hubristic fantasy in this. But he did not reject the fiction as
merely fiction. He wanted to know how to apply its raw appeal

properly, maturely. Though these first things of his could not reasonably be maintained in the realistic story of life and had ostensibly to be left behind, they remained still obstinately latent in the subsequent modification of their impulse. All the time, as he listened to his patients and imagined them, Sassall disguised his universal aspirations within his personal situation, hiding the great ambition within his small unglamorous provincial setting. That is why he had chosen to be a GP—because general practice is, like the realist novel, non-specialized, non-dramatic, almost unselectively wide-ranging across an ostensibly ordinary world containing nonetheless its hidden inner secrets. Significantly, there is one man in the village who understands Sassall, a man who is a writer and a novelist. He thinks Sassall brings to his patients the imagination of what might be called a practical novelist, a man transferring a novelist's imaginative skills into real life.

This is of course the story of John Berger's *A Fortunate Man* (1967), a book which I take to be a great test-case of the relation of literature and life. For it is a hybrid, a faction, an attempted ur-text which lays as honestly bare as it can the mix of fictional skill and factual subject that goes into the act of literary composition. It brings a novelist's insight to the real-life case study of a doctor, just as the novelist believes this doctor himself does in relation to his patients, so close and imaginatively translatable do the two vocations become here.

What a patient needs from a doctor, below the level of the common practical relationship, is *recognition*, says Berger. What is wrong with me? the patients say mutely, with their vulnerable eyes almost like children's again: What is it that you see? 'It would be a great mistake,' writes Berger, 'to "normalize" what I have just said by concluding that the patient wants a *friendly* doctor' or a *reassuring* doctor.[15] For this is a great example of when a literary language, rather than a normalizing language, is called for. 'Recognition' does not just mean hello to the regulars. It means making the patient feel properly recognized as an individual with a story, rather than a case. As he looks and listens and responds, Sassall seeks imaginatively to 'become' for a moment each person he sees. That is the novelist who for the inarticulate becomes 'the means of translating what they know into thoughts which they can think', lest too much of their emotional and introspective experience should remain unnamed, unrecognized, and unvalued even by themselves (p. 99). Especially when unhappy or scared, people ask of doctors what they used to ask of priests, for cure, pardon, and salvation wherever possible, for counsel and witness where not. That is the 'fortunate' burden for doctors—wonderful yet terrible—when the old categories break down, when meaning and help have to be sought anywhere they can be found, when the range of the medical has extended beyond the physical into the psychological, the environmental, the social, the political, and the spiritual. That is why, even in the need to feel useful and important, Sassall's Renaissance man begins to feel he has gone beyond his own strength and range, and all that is required is too much for him. Berger himself says of Sassall and his vocation, 'I cannot evaluate that work as I could easily do if he were a fictional character.... Now, by contrast, I am entirely at the mercy of realities I cannot encompass' (pp. 158–9). Some years after the publication of *A Fortunate Man*, his work became too much for Sassall in a sad and terrible ending.

Agents in the world

For Berger there is a whole range of human activities which derive from the same impulses or make practical the same faculties as those that also go into art and into literature in particular. A doctor may be a practical novelist; psychoanalysis, says one practitioner, is a kind of practical poetry through which people 'speak themselves'.[16] And it is not just that these human interventions are analogous to what goes into literature; it is also that they are enhanced by the use of literature as testing-ground and holding-ground, a model for the most complex human thinking about human things.

Literature is good for holding on to thoughts, that they may wait to find the right place for themselves in the world. That is what poetry says: there is a right word, a right thought on a particular occasion, demanded by need. And there are gaps that will be exposed in the world, opportune or danger points at which what has been stored will be needed in a new form. That storage is the great thought that F. W. H. Myers, one of the pioneers of psychology, offered in a book published after his death in 1903, called *Human Personality*. During our long evolutionary adaptation to new environments, he argued, there has been a continual displacement of 'the threshold' of consciousness. Certain faculties natural selection lifted above that threshold for the working purposes of everyday life, beginning with what is physically and materially most useful for survival. Others not called into consciousness as immediately useful were stored 'subliminally', below consciousness. It was these latent powers of which consciously we know little, that art in particular has kept alive for the race in extension of its potential capabilities. They emerge, shift, and mutate, finding new expressions within everyday life whenever something more subtly useful, or more than useful, is required there. So it is then, that in the great shifts of forms and frameworks, what might have gone on within the form of religion 200 years ago, and within education 100 years ago, may now have to be at work within what is so broadly and sometimes all too breezily called the realm of 'health' or 'well-being' (where indeed my own research unit is currently lodged). But Literature, and what literature stands for, is very good at continuing its work within frameworks to which it does not wholly accede. And if I am forced to name what it is that literature 'stands for' outside itself, even at this late stage, I will still want to try to give an example rather than some lame or pious definition.

My example comes from near the end of a little book by the Victorian literary critic R. H. Hutton on Sir Walter Scott, where Hutton is writing of the last seven years of Scott's life in which he struggled to honour the debts that resulted from the bankruptcy of the printing house in which he was a partner. In 1826 Scott found himself suddenly owing £117,000. Within two years he had earned £40,000 as a result of continuous writing work which virtually broke his health, though almost every day he had himself wheeled to his desk and the pen placed in his hand. His final debts, remaining at £54,000, were only paid off after his death in 1832 through life-insurance and the sale of his copyrights; but at some point towards the very end, the brain-disease which destroyed him made him think he had already paid off the obligation in full. Hutton had read all this in Lockhart's great biography. He then writes from an acute sense of paradox:

Till calamity came, Scott appeared to be a nearly complete natural man, and no more. Then first was perceived in him something above nature, something which could endure though every end in life for which he had fought so boldly should be defeated.[17]

Simply and straightforwardly trying to pay off his debts: Scott's greatness was to Hutton more visible in such adversity than in his long years of success as the author of *Waverley*. Yet Scott himself could never have been able to comfort himself with believing that: he could hardly write out of, and certainly not write about, that struggling, failing, equivocal achievement. That is one reason why the writer's biography exists—to write on his behalf and on behalf too of what is hidden within ordinary decent frameworks and limited material ends. 'The man was so much greater than the ends for which he strove,' Hutton concludes (p. 177). That sheer excess of character, of *being*, over those declared ends which nonetheless revealed as well as troubled it, speaks for all who would otherwise consider themselves lost and negligible, for want of being able to think of any new purpose to human life or any great one in their own. For Hutton, in the last days of Scott, this *is* the writer, and all that went into being the writer, only now increasingly without the gifts of writing. Such things are emphatically as Wordsworth said, 'sorrow, that is not sorrow...to hear of' (*The Prelude* (1805), 12.245–7). Which is true of much in literature, and of much from which I have quoted in this book.

Arguably Hutton underrates Scott the novelist, for there is in his work, within its dense intermixture of the natural and the historical, a struggling endeavour for more than easily exists in the empirical present. But Hutton is right to use biography to try to sense the distinctive signature, the personal mark or characteristic footprint left behind by the subject. So it is with Boswell on Johnson, J. W. Cross on George Eliot, Jessie Chambers on D. H. Lawrence, Nadezhda Mandelstam on her husband, Solomon Volkov on Shostakovich, or Norman Malcolm on Wittgenstein: in their differing ways they all give a non-specialist reader, who might not otherwise understand what was achieved, the personal feel of the subject as a surrounding aura to his or her work. They are works not of incidental background chat but of attempted translation. So too in his own effort with Scott, Hutton is acting as middle-man, learning through the help of the Victorian realist novel to do what we might call human thinking—thinking within the human without necessary recourse yet to any further transcendent framework of purpose or justification. He is in that the literary critic and biographer serving as translator, who knows that the content of life may at times constitute more than the forms in which it is found. Such is his role as a reader too: to find and save the scattered examples of resonant being, the traces of left-over life and unfinished purpose, which are in excess of explanation or outcome—whatever the genre and wherever they occurred.

In this Hutton was also what his contemporary, Matthew Arnold, would call an 'alien' in a sense very different from our own—what we might rather call 'agent'. Within each class of society and each social practice there are, wrote Matthew Arnold in *Culture and Anarchy* (1869), a number of aliens: that is, individuals led not by their class spirit but by a more broadly humane spirit, seeking to transcend narrow group interests. These aliens living amongst the conventionalists were precisely those who were *not*, in Marx's terms, alienated. In *The German Ideology* (1845–6), Marx had complained bitterly that too often doctors spoke only as doctors, lawyers as lawyers, and hardly ever as human beings separate from their enclosing professions. Arnold's aliens, however, were more like John Berger's John Sassall: from education and culture, and in particular from literature, they had access to levels of reference and meaning that could save them from being cogs in the company machine. They were like the agents of serious learning that Coleridge, a generation earlier, had called the clerisy: they functioned within the containing structures that they sought to change, without being of them. Likewise, the great Victorian realist novelists worked with the contemporary sense of what was real, to reveal further dimensions of meaning that were hidden or imprisoned inside it. This was the risk and the paradox: to operate within systems and institutions precisely to defy systemic institutionalization; to work within the world of books for the sake of what, beyond themselves, the books referred to.

It is not that I wholly endorse Matthew Arnold or wish to have us simply sign up again, from a later world, to the old cause offered by his defence of literature and culture. I favour the analysis offered by a contemporary commentator, S. H. Reynolds writing in *The*

Westminster Review (October 1863), who, comparing Arnold with Ruskin, spoke of Arnold as very much 'the critic', not least for having had to give up on his poetry; whereas Ruskin, more partial and less judicious, was always like a displaced or transferred 'artist'. That is what is wanted: not people who entirely fit within the form or the profession or the institution in which they are cast, but those who come from somewhere else, with personal vocations that speak to original purposes within secondary forms.

Burke and Nietzsche

Yet what Arnold is good at is the finding of his literary examples, whatever he then makes of them. One of the finest things in any literature, Arnold says in 'The Function of Criticism at the Present Time' (1864), is a piece he takes from Edmund Burke, writing at the very point at which (like Berger in *A Fortunate Man* refusing to let literature become safe and autonomous) the world of letters is vulnerable to the world itself. Bidding farewell to his life-purposes in some of the last pages he ever wrote, Burke is talking about his life-long opposition to the French Revolution and its continuing effects: 'The evil is stated, in my opinion, as it exists. The remedy must be where power, wisdom, and information, I hope, are more united with good intentions than they can be with me. I am done with the subject, I believe, for ever.' But then, right at the close, he imagines some great future development in later history which irresistibly emerges from the legacy of the French Revolution, and in retrospect proves the people who have thought as he did to have been blind and foolish and wrong after all:

If a great change is to be made in human affairs, the minds of men will be fitted to it; the general opinion and feelings will draw that way. Every fear, every hope will forward it; and then they who persist in opposing this mighty current in human affairs, will appear rather to resist the decrees of Providence itself, than the mere designs of men. They will not be resolute and firm, but perverse and obstinate.

Arnold thinks that this '*return* of Burke upon himself' is evidence of the sheer and almost beautiful disinterestedness involved in being able to think: the capacity to imagine a wholly different future in the midst of the present, to bear possible doubt in the midst of habitual conviction, and impartially to see another side even at grave cost to one's own. That admiration is justified, and the explicit inclusion of this extra consciousness, near the very point of mortality, is absolutely crucial; but I think the opposite is also true. That the great thing here is that Burke put himself, his beliefs, and his writings in a place where he knew that he—and they—could be wrong. Turning round upon the very framework within which he knew he must live out his remaining life, he still continued, loyal to himself, to 'return' also to his faith in what he had been. It was a belief all the greater because not stubbornly blind to its being utterly mistaken— where that possibility was not just a sceptical and playful but a fearful and painful thing. There is something more right about that stance in Burke than anything that might be proven for or against it in any future debate on the historical merits and vices of the French Revolution.

Open-mindedness, critical impartiality, pure disinterestedness, sceptical forewarning: it is not their value but their relative place in the order of things that is in dispute when I say that these cannot be an ultimate or an immediate goal. Even in Burke they are second thoughts, to deal with first ones. In Doris Lessing's *Marriages*, we may recall, the liberal queen of Zone Three needed to go down into the cruder realm of Zone Four, in order not to forget a fundamental need, however inconvenient to an easier idealism. So it is then that in his *Untimely Meditations* Nietzsche gives polemical warning against those who have read so much, learnt so much at second hand, that they have become over-conscious, over-doubtfully fair-minded, or overly critical in seeing every side of a question, and are paralysed as a result. In contrast, doubtless unfairly, those who want to do something in the world, says Nietzsche, are characteristically more personally partial and less eminently reasonable than that, even at the cost of being less generally just.

Imagine someone, says Nietzsche, for whom, seized by a vehement passion and undeterred by context or precedent, absolutely nothing exists but the subjective present. It is a vital state: 'No painter will paint his picture, no general achieve his victory, no people gain its freedom without having first desired and striven for it in an *un*historical condition.'[18] By such gambles, Nietzsche concludes, may history itself, even in its smallest sense, be made.

Granted: every such private aspiration could be no more than the sort of power-driven fantasy of ego of which Nietzsche is so frequently accused. Indeed, it risks being no more than that—unless and until it is externally achieved in a surge of action that remains ahead of past knowledge. Like the perhaps objectively untenable idea of one's unique experience, the personal belief nonetheless offers sufficient vitality to go forward upon. In that sense, 'the possible is not the antecedent of the actual but its consequence'.[19] Again, ontology comes before epistemology: 'Become who you are' was Nietzsche's call for realization.

There are pleasures and dangers and opportunities in what we might finally call fantasy, which indeed the emotional reading of literature and the licence of imagination may encourage. How could it be otherwise—as though the summoning of powers could be without hazard, invulnerable to the workings of the sub-conscious or unconscious? But I do not know the certain or separate difference between fantasy, imagination, excited thought, egoism, aspiration, the search for purpose—and so on and on and on, semantically. What I do believe is that we need the raw mix of such interrelated things, ahead of names, in the holding-ground of the careful and not undisciplined reading of literature. There thought, inseparable from language, may test that mix in a relatively safe area of recourse that exists nonetheless for the sake of the unsafe thinking that arises from it.

In the thick of seriously absorbed reading it is not merely what we *say* or *want* to think we are that is involved, but whatever is actually found and released in this imaginative model for the calls of unpremeditated experience. Yet it is still not fair-mindedness, or an empathic sense of otherness, or educationally expanded horizons that are the aim of the ethos here, however much sympathy, imagination, and the capacity to think from a second self are concomitantly important. It is rather that it might be better to have a world in which people felt free to be more authentically partial in themselves, knowing the risks and chances and without certainty of the outcome; in which the passionate demand for a more fundamentally personal life might have a voice that is not merely assertive but genuinely intent; in which occasions might still be found for the calling and exploring of individual attachment, purpose, need, good, and belief.

But all too often or too soon we are somehow tricked into an anonymity or a self-diminishment instead. It is the trick that life so easily played upon Thomas Hardy's Tess, for all her initial power of feeling:

Upon her sensations the whole world depended to Tess; through her existence all her fellow-creatures existed, to her. The universe itself only came into being for Tess on the particular day in the particular year in which she was born. (*Tess of the d'Urbervilles*, chapter 25)

The inevitable passions instinctively and involuntarily involved here are embodied evidence for us of 'the prior importance of my own world over *the* world'.[20] Tess is born into such embodiment, for better and worse, for change and continuity. And yet despite its status as a birthright, this basic biological core of phenomenal subjectivism does not last long for her. 'The Woman Pays' as Hardy puts it, and Tess's situation becomes no more than this, in her gathering shame at bearing an illegitimate child:

She might have seen that what had bowed her head so profoundly—the thought of the world's concern at her situation—was founded on an illusion. She was not an existence, an experience, a passion, a structure of sensations, to anybody but herself. To all humankind besides Tess was only a passing thought. (*Tess of the d'Urbervilles*, chapter 14)

Even Hardy's antidote is characteristically tough: remember that normatively nobody cares that much about you anyway, and certainly not as much as you care. But it is Tess's own subjective strength of feeling that is here ironically being turned back against her when she feels so ashamed of herself: this is how people may vulnerably dismiss, underrate, or denigrate themselves. The shift from being the centre of one's world to becoming one among many points on the world's circumference is a necessary development in an adult's psychological and moral acknowledgement of reality. But it is hard enough, sufficiently painful, without it destroying all remaining sense of that centre still inside oneself. Reading is one way that exists to get people out of that passive personal helplessness.

The work done on the inside
I don't know what else besides literature so much opens out the inside place in human beings. In Bernard Malamud's novel, Frank Alpine starts as the Thief, the masked accomplice caught up in the

mugging of Morris Bober in his grocery; returns to the store as the Assistant, trying to make secret reparation by working for little or nothing, though the petty thief in him keeps coming back to take from the till; and becomes finally the Grocer himself, after Bober's death, in support of the family. These are the forms he takes and struggles within. He has changed, he insists to others, even when he hasn't quite done so; he looks the same even when he is trying to be a different man. 'He could see out but nobody could see in.' It is the novel that sees in and reinforces the belief in that dimension.

In an imaginable future, in which the professionalization and institutionalization of health and faith and education might become less separately certain of themselves, there may be more room for what is stored inside people and inside the forms they work within. There may be more recognized need for the less predictable human thinking and feeling that comes from literature, itself so hiddenly central while so often publicly side-lined. In the meantime, as ever, literature offers its implicit holding-ground to its potential agents.

Readers maintain that ground, conserving and exploring and even perhaps extending it. If the place of writing and of reading is as I have described it, then 'the literary' is an extra dimension for human beings located essentially not within literature but between literature and life, awaiting further opportunities for establishing itself in an often depersonalized world. Readers are the personal carriers of that dimension and the representatives of that place.

The woman-queen in Doris Lessing's *The Marriages Between Zones Three, Four and Five* watches her husband-king trying to understand, as she too has had to, the marriage between his realm and hers, when finally he has found a place in which to think about it:

She said, 'If we were not to meant to understand each other, what are we doing here at all?'
From within deep thought, thought that was being protected, in fact, by his derisiveness, the stances of what he had always considered 'strength', he said, or breathed out, slowly, 'But what is it...I must understand...*what*? We have to understand...what...' he lapsed into silence, eyes fixed on a cup on the table. And she realized, with what delight and relief, that he was in fact operating from within that part of him which meant that he was open and ready for understandings to come into him—as she had been...'Here

we are soldiers...soldiers with no war...you are...you *are*...what are you?
What are we...*what are we for*...that's it, that's it...'
Like someone in sleep, he brought out these words, slow, toneless, each one
only a summary, a brief note or abstract, as it were of long processes of
inner thought....
He did not know what had just happened. Yet she could see on his face a
maturity that spoke for the deep processes that had been accomplished in
him.

This might be called self-transcendence if it wasn't that the so-called
self must be capable of it in the first place. It is not just that humans
could be two or three times more than they are, given the emotional, imaginative, and cognitive lift that they so often cannot give
themselves. It is rather that they could be operating at a whole new
level, however intermittently. It may be a person, but it may be an
institution or even a society that finds itself in that man's position
there, needing thoughts that are neglected, forgotten, or unrealized
within zones that have too long stayed closed.

Notes

1. Erich Auerbach, *Mimesis*, first published 1946, trans. W. R. Trask
   (Princeton: Princeton University Press, 1968), 11–12.
2. Søren Kierkegaard, *Fear and Trembling* (1843), trans. A. Hannay (London:
   Penguin, 1985), 74–5 (adapted).
3. Søren Kierkegaard, *The Sickness Unto Death* (1849), trans. H. V. and
   E. H. Hong (Princeton: Princeton University Press, 1990), 94.
4. Stanley Middleton, *Valley of Decision* (London: Hutchinson, 1985),
   211–12.
5. Marcel Proust, *On Reading Ruskin*, trans. and ed. J. Autret, W. Burford,
   and P. J. Wolfe (New Haven: Yale University Press, 1987), 109.
6. The examples are Alasdair MacIntyre's in *The Tasks of Philosophy* (Cambridge: Cambridge University Press, 2006), i. 3.
7. Wole Soyinka, *The Man Died* (1972) (London: Arrow Books, 1985), 88–9,
   94.
8. Les Murray, *The Paperbark Tree* (London: Carcanet, Minerva, 1992), 259.
9. <www.jstor.org/discover/10.2307/1343768?uid=3738032&uid=2129
   &uid=2&uid=70&uid=4&sid=47698831445157>.
10. Stanislas Dehaene, *Reading in the Brain* (London: Penguin, 2010), 212.
11. See Maryanne Wolf, *Proust and the Squid* (Cambridge: Icon Books, 2008),
    especially chapters 2 and 3; Joseph Gold, *The Story Species* ((Ontario:
    Fitzhenry & Whiteside, 2002), chapters 1 and 2 and pp. 178–81.

12. 'Critic/Reader', in *Real Voices on Reading*, ed. Philip Davis (London: Macmillan, 1997), 3–37.

13. Michael Wood, *Literature and the Taste of Knowledge* (Cambridge: Cambridge University Press, 2005), 126–7, where he argues of literary works acting as parables: 'We can't make sense of them if we don't find this scene [of application], if we don't apply them somewhere, if we don't find a connection for them in the world we inhabit. In the different worlds we inhabit.'

14. Joseph Conrad, 'Typhoon', chapter 3; hereafter cited as 'Typhoon'.

15. John Berger, *A Fortunate Man*, first published 1967 (London: Vintage, 1997), 68–9; hereafter cited as Berger.

16. Adam Phillips interviewed in The Economist <http://www.economist.com/blogs/prospero/2012/03/qa-adam-phillips>.

What do you see as the relationship between psychoanalysis and poetry? The most obvious link is that they are both linguistic arts. Freud suggests not exactly that we speak in poetry, because poetry has line-endings, but that we potentially speak with the type of incisiveness and ambiguity that we're most used to finding in poetry. So, to put it slightly differently: the reading of poetry would be a very good training for a psychoanalyst.

In the preface to 'On Flirtation' you call psychoanalysis a 'kind of practical poetry'—can you elaborate on this? On the one hand, psychoanalysis is practical in the sense that there is an attempt to solve a problem, or to cure somebody, or at least to address their suffering. But the other thing that psychoanalysis does is that the project is to enable somebody to speak. It's the attempt to create the conditions in which somebody can speak themselves as fully as possible. It is as though Freud invented a setting or a treatment in which people could not exactly speak the poetry that they are, but that they could articulate themselves as fully as they are able.

17. R. H. Hutton, *Sir Walter Scott* (London: Macmillan, 1887 edition), 176. Hereafter cited as Hutton.

18. Friedrich Nietzsche, *Untimely Meditations*, first published 1893, trans. R. J. Hollingdale (Cambridge: Cambridge University Press, 1983), 64 ('The Uses and Disadvantages of History for Life').

19. Roberto Mangabeira Unger, *The Self Awakened: Pragmatism Unbound* (Cambridge, Mass.: Harvard University Press, 2007), 61.

20. Philip Fisher, *The Vehement Passions* (Princeton: Princeton University Press, 2002), 249.

Permissions

Short Bibliography

Note: Many of the works that have most influenced this book are referred to in the main body of the text and the endnotes. The following non-fictional works are, perhaps, some of the less obvious texts to which, eclectically, I am indebted and which may be useful as further reading.

Karl Barth, *Evangelical Theology: An Introduction*, 1963, trans. Grover Foley (Grand Rapids, Mich.: Eerdmans, 1979).

W. R. Bion, *Attention and Interpretation* (London: Tavistock Publications, 1970).

Martin Buber, *I and Thou*, trans. Walter Kaufmann (Edinburgh: T. & T. Clark, 1970).

Joseph Gold, *Read for your Life* (Ontario: Fitzhenry & Whiteside, 1990).

Joseph Gold, *The Story Species* (Ontario: Fitzhenry & Whiteside, 2002).

Marion Milner, *A Life of One's Own*, 1934 (London: Virago, 1986).

Marion Milner, *An Experiment in Leisure*, 1937 (London: Virago, 1986).

Iris Murdoch, *Metaphysics as a Guide to Morals* (London: Chatto & Windus, 1992).

Thomas Nagel, *Mortal Questions* (Cambridge: Cambridge University Press, 1979).

Robert Ornstein, *Multimind* (Boston: Houghton Mifflin Company, 1986).

Catherine Pickstock, *After Writing* (Oxford: Blackwell, 1998).

Oliver Sacks, *A Leg to Stand On* (London: Picador, 1986).

Roberto Mangabeira Unger, *Passion* (New York: The Free Press, Macmillan, 1984).

A. N. Whitehead, *Process and Reality*, 1929 (New York: The Free Press, Macmillan, 1978).

Index